pg. 1

pg. 2

Digital Photography: Book 1
Mastering Digital Cameras:
An Illustrated Guidebook

By Al Judge

Sedona, Arizona
Copyright © 2013 by Al Judge

Edition 2, March 2014
Corrected Minor Typos and Links

Table of Contents

Introduction   **6**
  My Approach & Philosophy   8
  What to Expect From This Book   10

Chapter One: Camera Basics   **12**
  Pinhole Cameras   12
  Film Cameras   14
  Digital Cameras   21
  All about Lenses   24
  What is an Aperture?   27
  What is a Shutter?   29
  The Digital SLR Camera   31
  Some Things to Remember   39
  Photographic Terms Introduced in this Chapter   40

Chapter Two – Before you Buy a Camera ...   **43**
  Digital Camera Sensors   43
  File Formats   45
  Some Things to Remember   47
  Photographic Terms Introduced in this Chapter   47

Chapter Three – Your Digital Camera Choices   **49**
  Point–and–Shoot (P&S)   49
  Compact Cameras   53
    Nikon Coolpix P510   54
    Canon G10   60
    Olympus Pen E-PL1   61
    Canon EOS M   62
  DSLR Cameras   64
    Canon Rebel T4i   66
    Canon 5D Mark III   70
  Nikon D3100   72
  Medium-Format Cameras   74
  Large-Format Cameras   75
  Camera Comparisons   78
  Some Things to Remember   79
  Photographic Terms Introduced in this Chapter   79

Chapter Four: Interchangeable Lenses   **80**
  Types of Lenses   81
  Effective Focal Length   88
  Aperture Values of Lenses   90
  Understanding Lens Designations   92

Nikon (Nikkor) Lenses 97
Sigma Lenses 98
Tamron Lenses 99
Tokina Lenses 99
Zeiss Lenses 100
Some Things to Remember 100
Photographic Terms Introduced in this Chapter 101

Chapter Five: Understanding the Exposure Triangle 103

What is ISO? 103
Aperture 104
Shutter Speed 108
Exposure Stops 109
Conclusion 110
Some Things to Remember 111
Photographic Terms Introduced in this Chapter 113

Chapter Six: White Balance and Other Digital Camera Controls 114

White Balance 114
Auto-Focus 115
Auto-Exposure 116
Remote Shutter Release 119
Color Space 120
Highlight Tone Priority 121
Auto Lighting Optimizer 121
Additional Information 122
Photographic Terms Introduced in this Chapter 123

Chapter Seven: Parting Thoughts and Recommendations 124

Glossary: Photography Speak 127

Canon Lenses 132
Nikon (Nikkor) Lenses 133
Sigma Lenses 134
Tamron Lenses 135
Tokina Lenses 135
Zeiss Lenses 136

Introduction

This is the first of at least three books in the ***Digital Photography*** Series. These books are quite comprehensive but are also appropriate for absolute beginners because they require no previous knowledge of photography. Book 2 will cover the **Art of Photography** and Book 3 will cover **Photo Editing**.

Before we begin our journey into the world of Digital Photography, I thought it might be helpful to take a moment to look at where the journey might lead.

One of the wonderful things about the Internet is that we get to meet people and share experiences with those people in a way that was not possible just a few years ago. As a by-product of writing these books about Digital Photography, I had the pleasure of meeting someone whom I would never have met otherwise. Her name is Darlene Jansen (http://www.darlenejansen.smugmug.com/) and I personally believe that she is an exceptionally talented photographer. With her permission, I have used some of her images in this book to demonstrate several points.

© Darlene Jansen 2012

Note the color and detail in these images. They are "tack sharp" (a photography term), the color is exquisite, the composition draws you in and brings your attention to the subject, the background enhances the image rather than distracting from it. All of these things require a solid mastery of the equipment used. But what really sets them apart is that they convey a sense of awe and wonder. I get a feeling of joy and excitement in my gut every time I see images like these. I am transported to another place – a happy place – a place where the stress of everyday life does not exist. This is the magic of art in any form.

© Darlene Jansen 2012

Photography can enhance your life in more ways than you ever imagined. You will become aware of light and how it affects your world like never before. You will begin to see the beauty in the mundane. You will feel more a part of everything, and you will focus more on the moment and less on the past and future. In brief, you will become "more present." It is wonderfully liberating.

Here's an idea for an interesting experiment: Observing the work of others is always a great way to learn more about photography. I make it a point to look at new photos every day. So do yourself a favor and go to Flickr or a website like Darlene Jansen's (http://www.darlenejansen.smugmug.com/). On Darlene's site, there are hundreds of photos divided into categories and there is also a "Most Popular" category. Look at the photos in each group and write down the name or a description of your "Best of Group" picks. Save your list for another exercise at the end of this book.

There are several benefits to this exercise:

Comparing images will make you more conscious of details and why you like certain features or characteristics.

You will become more aware of what grabs your attention.

You will experience a mini vacation.

At the end of the book, I will remind you to get your list out and look at your picks again. You should see things differently by then. This exercise should also give you some insight into your natural instincts. When I look at photos that I took 30 years ago, I am often surprised by the quality of the composition and other details, considering that I knew so little about composition back then.

Digital Cameras are everywhere today. Between smart phones and compact point-and-shoot cameras, most people always have a camera with them. The technology has advanced so much in the last decade that even smart phones take great snapshots. There is, however, a whole world of photography that goes beyond snapshots. You can't capture images like the two you have just seen with a point-and-shoot camera. You need to have more control over the process, and equipment that is designed for the job.

In the pages that follow, I will gently walk you through the sometimes confusing and intimidating world of digital photography. As we go forward, I will do my best to make the path clear and the journey pleasant. No prior knowledge of photography will be required of you, only your time and attention. If I do my job right, you will arrive at the end of this book with a clear understanding of how digital cameras work as well as an understanding of your options in Digital Cameras and Lenses.

Now that you know where we are headed, let's get on with it.

My Approach & Philosophy

For me, time is my most valuable asset. I only have so much left, I don't know how much is left, and I really hate wasting it. With that in mind, I really appreciate it when I read a non-fiction book that is Content-Dense. By that I mean, very little wasted rhetoric. A certain amount of non-specific dialog is necessary to establish rapport with readers, but then I get anxious to learn something and hate fluff and colorful banter that doesn't enhance my learning.

Because of this personal bias, I tend to write books that are Content-Dense, even when they involve real life stories to illustrate key points. This book is no different.

My goal is to help you move from your current level of photographic expertise to total control and confidence in the most efficient way possible.

Throughout this book, I will often use initial caps, all caps, bold fonts, and italics for emphasis. With so much content, I want to be certain that key points are recognized as such.

I can't guarantee great works of art by tomorrow, but I can give you the **tools** to achieve that goal in the time it takes to read this series of books.

That is not to say that this series alone will teach you everything that you need to know about Digital Photography. I know some very successful Master Photographers who still read about photography every day. So, if they are still learning new things after 30 or 40 years in the profession, there is a limit to what I can actually cover effectively in a series of books. With that in mind, I have tried to cover the most important information in enough detail that it will accelerate your learning significantly.

After writing my first draft of this book, I read some best sellers on the topic. I wanted to be certain that I had something to bring to the. The thing that seemed to be most absent was visualization aids.

Like most people, I understand things by visualizing them. I form an image in my mind when people explain something, and I use that image to follow the discussion. If my image is erroneous, I will have a difficult time following the discussion. If I am unable to modify my mental image enough to get the points being made, I go elsewhere and research the topic until I have enough information to complete the puzzle. In my own personal journey in the world of photography, I have discovered that Photographic Terms are commonly used without definition and that parts of the camera are often referred to as if we are all technicians who could repair a camera in our sleep.

I have decided to take a slightly different approach than others have in writing these books. I believe that **if you understand how a camera works, everything else about photography will make more sense.** I could simply tell you that you need a large aperture setting when you make portraits of your spouse and kids. I could also tell you that you need a small aperture setting for your landscape photos. This is what most books on photography will tell you.

But what if you understood *why* these settings work so well and had a mental image of *how* these settings affect the light entering the camera?

With this understanding, **every image that you capture will teach you something of real significance – not just give you a vague idea of what works and what doesn't.**

With this in mind, I have made these books Image-Intense. With the use of numerous images, I can make the discussion less technical, and you will have the same image in your mind as I do. This should improve communication and give you a solid base for moving forward. I promise to make it as painless as I possibly can. Without this step, it is difficult to clearly describe the different categories of cameras and even more difficult to compare different models in the same category. But beyond that, **until you understand a camera, you will** not really understand how to use it to its fullest potential. You will be learning by trial and error and "shooting in the dark."

What to Expect from This Book

Whether you are thinking about purchasing your first digital camera, upgrading your current equipment, or just want to know more about photography, there should be plenty of valuable information in these pages. I have challenged myself to carefully review every statement to be certain that it is written clearly and in a way that does not assume any photographic experience on the part of the reader. From personal experience, this is what I have found most frustrating about even the best photography books. Invariably, a term or concept that I have never heard of before is mentioned as casually as if it were universally known. I promise that I will make every effort to avoid undefined terms. If I slip up, please let me know (ajudex@hotmail.com). I welcome and appreciate any constructive criticism; it helps me to improve my books.

My plan is to build a solid foundation, one topic at a time, until a thorough yet understandable presentation has developed.

We will start by presenting an overview of photography that will facilitate understanding in later chapters. Next, we will look at your camera options and why I believe that a Digital Single Lens Reflex (DSLR) camera is your best choice. And yes, I will not only define and explain DSLR, but will use photos and illustrations to take the mystery out of camera selection and usage. After we have completed this overview of cameras and photography, I will define and explain every important term and concept that you need to know to make an informed decision about your photographic future.

In just a few hours, you should not only know the basics of photography but feel confident in your ability to capture some beautiful images.

I have used numerous (roughly 120) images to illustrate key points, so that they are more understandable as well as memorable. Every important term or concept will be highlighted with **BOLD CAPS** so that you can quickly and easily find important information when you need to refresh your memory about a particular topic.

Your pictures will improve dramatically if you are relaxed and having fun rather than being stressed out over a camera that you find intimidating to use.

Photography is all about recording images. This might sound obvious, but it really goes beyond the obvious. There is a strictly mechanized aspect to it. This is the focus of this book – *Book 1: Mastering Digital Cameras*.

There is also the artistic aspect of photography. This will be the focus of **Book 2: The Art of Photography**, in which I will present examples of key photographic concepts and camera adjustments. The more comfortable you are with your equipment, the more likely you will benefit from this part of the series and be able to capture the emotion of the moment as well as the reality.

Book 3: Photo Editing will continue the artistic theme established in Book 2 and enhance your ability to create art rather than mere snapshots. Photo Editing is the digital equivalent of the Darkroom that was so much a part of film photography and is absolutely essential if you want to move beyond Point-and-Shoot Photography. Until you edit an image, it is just a snapshot. It becomes a work of art when you take control and modify the image to convey an emotion or share a moment of wonder.

Chapter One: Camera Basics

A number of Photographic terms will be introduced in this chapter. New terms will be repeated in a brief glossary at the end of each chapter in the order that they appeared. These same terms and others will also appear at the end of the book – **Glossary: Photography Speak** – in *alphabetical* order so that you can easily and quickly refresh your memory when these terms come up again.

I know that a lot of people will say, "I don't care how a camera works; I just want to know how to take better pictures." To those people, I ask that you bear with me. You will take better pictures sooner if you understand how a camera works. Without this understanding you may find yourself being misled and misinformed by people who think they know more than they do.

A general understanding of how cameras work makes it much easier to explain your options with regard to purchasing a camera. Also, adjusting Aperture, Shutter Speed, and ISO will also be easier to explain. Overall, this chapter will help you to see the big picture.

Modern cameras have so many settings and capabilities that they can be quite overwhelming at times. Some people are so intimidated by the technology that they barely scratch the surface when it comes to their camera's capabilities. The good news is, the basic principles of operation are really quite simple. If you understand these things, even the most sophisticated and complex equipment will be easier to understand and operate.

Pinhole Cameras

Figure 1.1

This image is the result of a twenty minute exposure with a pinhole camera.

Ewan McGregor - Wikipedia Commons Image

Most people are surprised to learn that you don't even need a lens to make a camera. Pinhole cameras have been around for centuries (**Figure 1.3**). These are basically light-tight boxes (**Figure 1.2**) with a very small hole on one side. An inverted image is projected into the box onto the side opposite the hole.

The image is inverted because light travels in straight lines from the object to the image surface. Points at the top of the object project to the bottom of the image and points at the bottom of the object project to the top of the image.

If the back of the box is translucent – like a piece of paper – the object can be viewed by looking at the back of the box from the outside. This is one way to safely observe a solar eclipse.

If a photographic recording medium – like film – is placed at the back of the box, you have a camera. If the photographic medium is an electronic sensor, you have a DIGITAL camera.

Figure 1.2

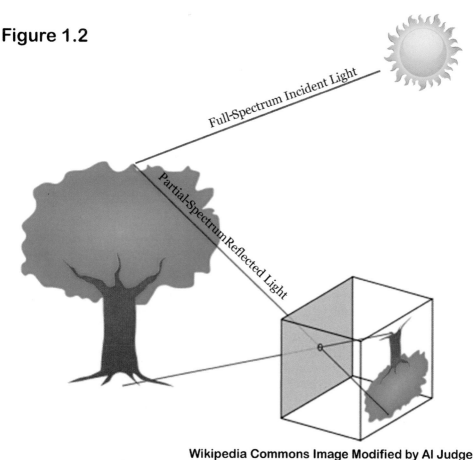

Wikipedia Commons Image Modified by Al Judge

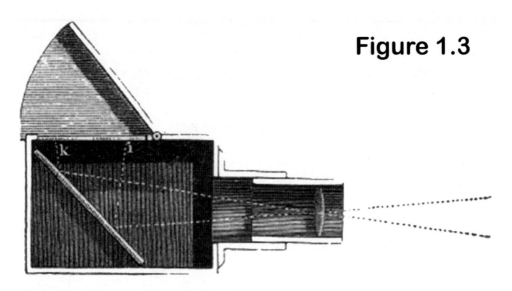

Figure 1.3

Image of Pinhole Camera first published in 1877.

Film Cameras

FILM CAMERAS created the way we think about and talk about cameras, so even if Digital Photography is our topic, understanding some of the history of film cameras is helpful.

Until about 1950, camera usage was clearly divided into consumer cameras and professional cameras. These devices looked different, operated differently, and were miles apart in cost.

In general, a consumer camera was small and relatively inexpensive. It required little or no expertise. If you could aim it at something and push a button, you had a snapshot – a visual record of what was happening at the time.

Film for these consumer cameras came in rolls (**Figure 1.4**) that were easy to load and contained a certain number of **FRAMES** per roll. A frame is the area of the film where one image can be recorded. So, a roll with 20 frames meant that you could take 20 snapshots before you had to change the film. You would then take the film to a photo shop or drugstore where it would be sent away for developing. A week or two later, you would return to the store and pick up your prints. It was always a surprise to see your pictures because most people had no concept of photographic principles and results could rarely be anticipated.

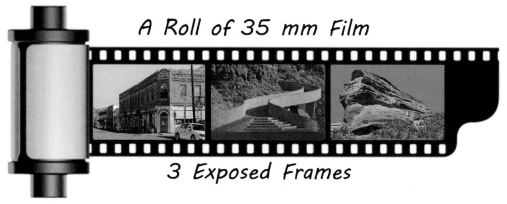

A Roll of 35 mm Film

3 Exposed Frames

Figure 1.4

©iStockphoto·com/pavlen
Modified by Al Judge

Professional photography was a world apart from the consumer approach to photography. The equipment was large, expensive, heavy, and required a great deal of skill to operate. Images were recorded on glass plates (like x-ray plates) that were inserted into the back of the camera and exposed one by one. The camera was mounted on a tripod, mostly because it was too heavy and bulky to be hand-held. It could take hours to set up the camera, make the adjustments, and capture a single image. After the shoot, the photographer would develop **NEGATIVES** from the plates in his **DARKROOM**. The process involved soaking the glass plate in several solutions, rinsing it thoroughly with water, coating it with varnish, and letting it air dry.

Figure 1.5

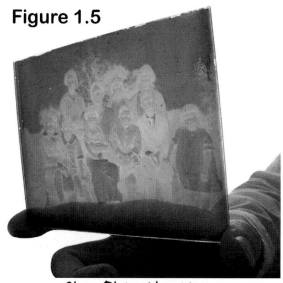

Glass Plate Negative
Source: http://bender-photo·com/wordpress/?cat=1&paged=2

Figure 1.6

Contact Print from Negative

A Negative (**Figure 1.5**) is a photographic master print from which Positive (**Figure 1.6** Normal) Prints are made. The tonal values of the Negative are the exact opposite of the Positive or Print. In other words, white appears as black on the negative and black appears as white.

To create a glass plate Negative, a glass plate is coated with a chemical solution that contains Silver Nitrate. When it is exposed to light the Silver absorbs the light and turns dark. The more light that is absorbed the darker the Silver gets, until some parts of the glass plate coating turn black. So, the brightest light in the image becomes the darkest areas of the negative.

When a short burst of light passes through a Negative and is projected onto white photosensitive paper, the dark areas of the negative will block some of the light and the light areas will receive the full intensity of the light. When the photo paper is **DEVELOPED** in chemical solutions, the areas with the most exposure to the light will be the darkest. The result is a Positive print. The distance between the negative and the photo paper determines the size of the print. An Enlarger (**Figure 1.6 A**) is a device that allows the photographer precise control over the print size.

Figure 1.6 A

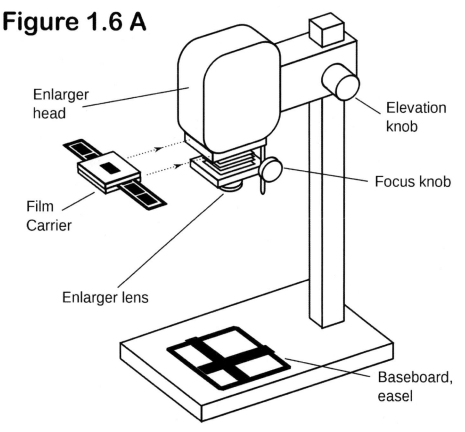

Enlarger head

Elevation knob

Focus knob

Film Carrier

Enlarger lens

Baseboard, easel

©Wikipedia Commons Image/Darkroom_Enlarger.svg/Ggia

Glass plate negatives were also used to make **CONTACT PRINTS** – also in the Darkroom. The Negative was placed face down on a piece of light-sensitive photo paper and exposed to light for a limited amount of time. The exact amount of time selected was part of the art of printing images and critical to the end result. The exposed photo paper was then developed using three trays of different chemical solutions. The result was a contact print, so named because the negative was in direct contact with the paper when it was exposed to light as part of the developing process. In this case, the print was the same size as the Negative.

Color negatives show the same type of reversed tonal effects as well as color reversals – complementary colors.

Negatives can be glass plates, photographic film, or digital files.

We will talk about Digital Negatives in ***Book 3: Photo Editing***.

Figure 1.7 Ansel Adams in his Darkroom

http://thedigitalvisual·com/a-rare-tour-of-ansel-adamss-home-and-darkroom

The photo above (**Figure 1.7**) shows Ansel Adams in his Darkroom. When developing negatives or contact prints, there is no light in a Darkroom except a dim red light bulb.

Every image printed required the use of toxic chemicals and hours of work. A negative could only produce a few hundred images before it lost its clarity. Making additional negatives was another important part of the process if the photographer hoped to sell more than 200 copies of an image.

Glass plates were the preferred photographic medium of professionals into the 1970's. They were used for scientific research – like star charts – until the 1990's. The images recorded on glass plates were sharper than those recorded on film because the glass plates were extremely flat and smooth. Film could not be held perfectly flat in any camera so that there would always be a slight blur due to the barely detectable warping of the film. Glass plates were also preferred for Astrophotography because they are extremely sensitive to light. Through photography, many heavenly objects were observed for the first time. The light was just too dim to be seen by human vision, even with a telescope.

The darkroom was so critical to professional photography that Masters of Photography, like Ansel Adams, insisted on personally developing and printing every image. It has often been said that much more could be accomplished in the Darkroom than behind the camera. Adams was still working in the Darkroom until a few days before his death in 1984 at the age of 82.

Around 1950, some Japanese companies started producing cameras that bridged the gap between consumers and professionals and forever changed the way we take pictures. These cameras were designed around 35 mm film and the Single Lens Reflex (**SLR**) approach – something that we will talk about very soon. Like the professional cameras, you could change lenses and make numerous adjustments. Like the consumer cameras, they were small enough and light enough to hold in your hand and take pictures without a tripod.

Although the first 35 mm cameras were built in the 1920's, they had limited success because they were quite expensive. It was the SLR design of the 1950's that changed the market forever.

35 mm SLR Film Camera Cut-Away

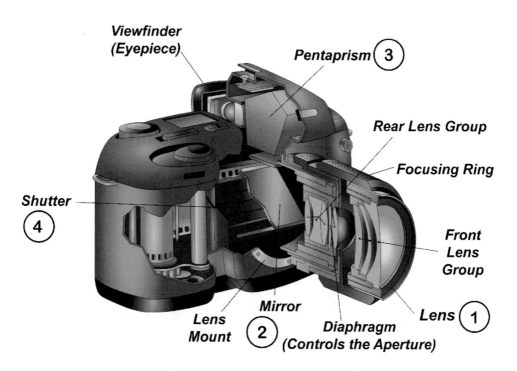

Figure 1.8

Wikipedia Commons Image/ Anuskafm
Modified by Al Judge

We will be talking more about the SLR design in the next section, but before we go on, please note the location of the Pentaprism in **Figure 1.8**. This is a special type of lens that flips the image coming through the Camera Lens so that the photographer sees the image right-side-up when she looks through the Viewfinder.

All SLR (Single Lens Reflex) cameras – Film and Digital – have four important characteristics in common:

1) Interchangeable Lenses. Note the Lens Mount in the illustration.
2) A Mirror between the Shutter and the Camera Lens that diverts the image to the Viewfinder for composing and focusing the shot.
3) A Pentaprism for flipping the image before it reaches the Eyepiece.
4) A Curtain Shutter that is closed except for those brief periods of taking a photo.

The film used in SLR cameras was basically the same 35 mm film that had been used to make movies since 1909. With some minor changes, it was repackaged into rolls like consumer film for still photography. The 35 mm format quickly gained wide acceptance because it was recognized as a great compromise between cost and image quality. The camera was small enough and light enough that it offered advantages to the professional that were previously unavailable.

Landscape photography no longer required hauling heavy and bulky equipment over rough terrain. The photographer could go places that he or she had never before considered. For the consumer, the moderate cost opened up a whole new world of photographic possibilities.

By the middle of the 1950's the camera market was divided into point-and-shoot cameras for average consumers, 35 mm cameras for photographic enthusiasts and professionals, and **MEDIUM- AND LARGE-FORMAT** cameras for professionals and very rich amateurs.

Figure 1.9

A 4X5 Large-Format Film Camera

©iStockphoto·com/LargeFormat4X5

Medium- and Large-Format (**Figure 1.9**) refers to the size of the film that is used in these cameras. The camera above captures an image that is 4 inches by 5 inches. For comparison, a 35 mm camera records an image that is slightly smaller than 1.5 inch by 1.0 inch. This means that the image captured by this large-format camera is about 14 times the size of the 35 mm image. This results in images that can be enlarged significantly and still remain sharp. They also capture more of the fine details. The drawback is price. It is not unusual to pay $20,000 to $50,000 for a camera of this type.

In 1999, Nikon introduced the first **DIGITAL SLR (DSLR)** camera made by a major manufacturer. Its design was based on the 35 mm film camera. The transition was further facilitated by the fact that it looked like a 35 mm camera. By 2002, the film camera market was dying, and most consumer films have since been discontinued.

Digital Cameras

The primary difference between a film camera and a digital camera is that in digital cameras the image is recorded by a photosensitive **SENSOR** (**Figure 1.10**) rather than film. The image file created by the Sensor is then stored on a memory card.

Figure 1.10

Photographic Sensor

Digital images are like a huge mosaic. Mosaics (**Figure 1.11**) are made up of many pieces of glass, stone, or other material. Likewise, digital images are made from many Picture Elements or Pixels (**PI**cture **EL**ements).

Figure 1.11

A Mosaic from the floor of an ancient palace.

©Wikipedia Commons Image/Cordanrad

Irano-Roman floor mosaic detail from the palace of Shapur I at Bishapur

The SENSOR of a Digital Camera has millions of PHOTOSITES. These are incredibly small depressions (cavities) that collect photons of light. Each photosite is programmed to record the quantity of a particular color of the light that strikes it during the process of capturing a single image. In **Figure 1.12A**, note that there are more Green boxes than either Red or Blue. This is because the human eye is more sensitive to Green light than Red or Blue, so more Green Photosites are used.

Figure 1.12 A

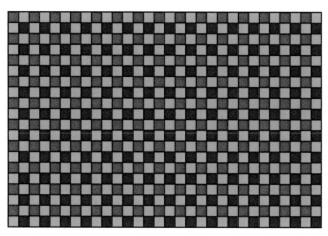

A Portion of a Photographic Sensor

The Color of Each Square indicates the Color of light that it traps. It does not indicate the actual appearance of the Sensor.

The Sensor then uses this data to create PIXELs (PIcture ELements) that form the mosaic pieces that result in a digital image.

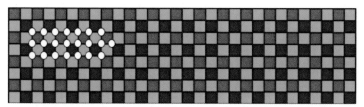

The White Dots in the image above illustrate how pixels are created from photosites in one particular algorithm. In this case, each pixel (white dot) is based on the data from the four photosites that it touches. This approach is not universal among Sensor Manufacturers.

Figure 1.12 B

There is not a direct one-to-one relationship between Photosites and Pixels. The way in which the pixels are generated from the photosite data is beyond the scope of this book and quite complex. **Figure 1.12 B** illustrates the beginning of one particular algorithm for creating Pixels from photosites. There are additional steps in the process that result in more Pixels.

The complete image recorded by a typical sensor might contain 16 million pixels, or 16 megapixels. The clarity and detail of an image is directly related to the number of pixels. More pixels = More Detail = Sharper Image.

This does not mean that all 16 Megapixel cameras are created equal. The actual image quality is also dependent upon the overall physical size of the sensor.

Sensors in DSLR cameras are 20 to 40 times the size of sensors in entry-level point-and-shoot cameras.

This means that each photosite is also much larger. A larger photosite is more capable of capturing low-intensity light as well as subtle tones and colors. We will talk more about Sensors later in the book, but for now the important point is that the size of the camera's **SENSOR** is one of the two primary factors contributing to overall image quality. The other critical factor is the **LENS**. For now, just remember:

The primary difference between a film camera and a digital camera is that in digital cameras the image is recorded by a photosensitive SENSOR rather than film.

SENSOR size and LENS quality are the two most important factors affecting image quality.

All about Lenses

Let's start with a simple example and then add to it.

For the illustrations in this chapter which involve light passing through a lens, assume the photographer is on the right and the objects being photographed are on the left.

In its simplest form, a LENS is a piece of curved glass that refracts (bends) light rays in a manner that causes them to converge or diverge. For the lens below **(Figure 1.13)**, the rays converge to a single point called the **FOCAL POINT**.

Figure 1.13

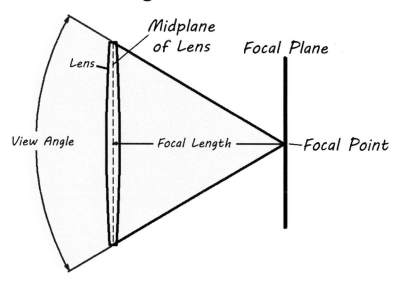

The distance from the Midplane (center of the thickness) of the lens to the Focal Point is called the **FOCAL LENGTH** of the Lens.

The **FOCAL PLANE** is a plane that is parallel to the midplane of the lens and contains the Focal Point.

Another important characteristic of a lens is its **VIEW ANGLE (Figure 1.14)** or **ANGLE OF VIEW**. This is the expanse, or angular view, that is visible through the lens. It can be measured horizontally, vertically, or diagonally.

Figure 1.14

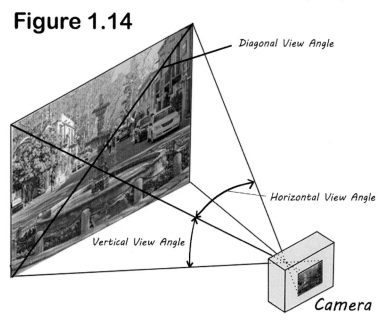

In real life, all lenses have defects called **ABERRATIONS**. For example, light rays might not all converge at a single point, or light waves of different colors might converge at different points. By stacking a number of simple lenses along a common axis, these defects can be significantly reduced or eliminated. The result is a **COMPOUND LENS**.

In this book, a compound lens is assumed when LENS is mentioned. In photographic terms, the term LENS implies a Compound Lens.

On a few occasions, the term Lens will be used to describe Simple Lenses in order to simplify technical discussions. In these cases, an illustration will show a Simple Lens.

The following chart (**Figure 1.15**) shows the shape of some common simple lenses.

Figure 1.15

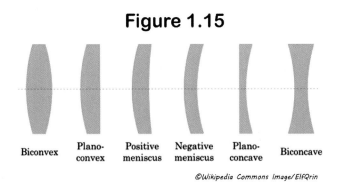

©Wikipedia Commons Image/ElfQrin

Figure 1.16 and **Figure 1.17** below illustrate some possible combinations of simple lenses to create compound lenses. The thin, vertical partition in each of these images is the **DIAPHRAGM**. We will discuss the diaphragm a little later in this chapter. The light from the object being photographed is moving from the left, through the Lens, toward the Sensor on the right.

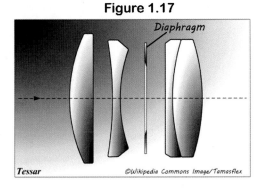

Figure 1.16 — Angenieux — ©Wikipedia Commons Image/Tamasflex

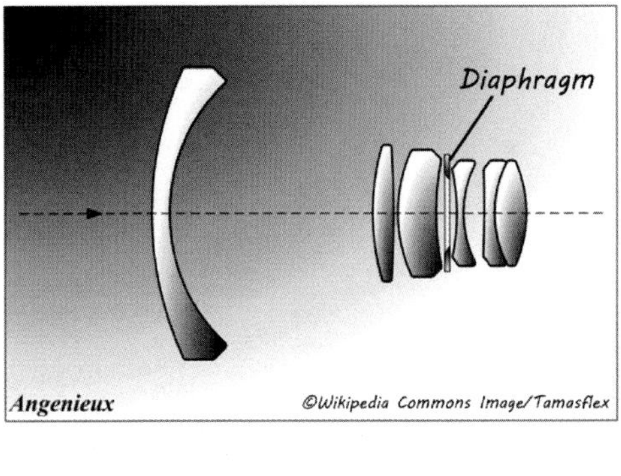

Figure 1.17 — Tessar — ©Wikipedia Commons Image/Tamasflex

A Compound Lens will have a Focal Length just like a Simple Lens.

We'll talk more about Lenses a little later, but for now, just remember:

A camera LENS is a collection of simple lenses with a common axis that work together to create a sharp image. Some important characteristics of a LENS are FOCAL LENGTH and VIEW ANGLE.

A **PENTAPRISM (Figure 1.18)** is a very special type of lens used in SLR and DSLR Cameras to invert an image. It is the reason that a photographer sees the image right-side-up when he looks through the viewfinder of an SLR or DSLR camera. Most people take this for granted, but most Large-Format and some Medium-Format cameras still display the image in an inverted position on the focusing screen.

Figure 1.18

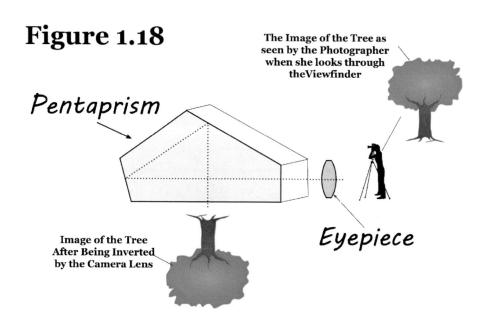

The Image of the Tree as seen by the Photographer when she looks through theViewfinder

Pentaprism

Image of the Tree After Being Inverted by the Camera Lens

Eyepiece

Wikipedia Commons Image - Modified by Al Judge

A Pentaprism is a lens that inverts an image. The dotted line shows the path of the light through the lens. This lens is used to flip the image that is projected through the camera lens so that it appears right-side up to the photographer.

What is an Aperture?

APERTURE simply means hole. The pinhole of the Pinhole Camera is its Aperture. Unlike the Pinhole Camera, most other cameras have an Aperture that can be varied in size. As seen in **(Figure 1.19)**, the size of the hole is determined by the movement of several blades. The opening can be opened and closed much like the Iris of the human eye.

Figure 1.19

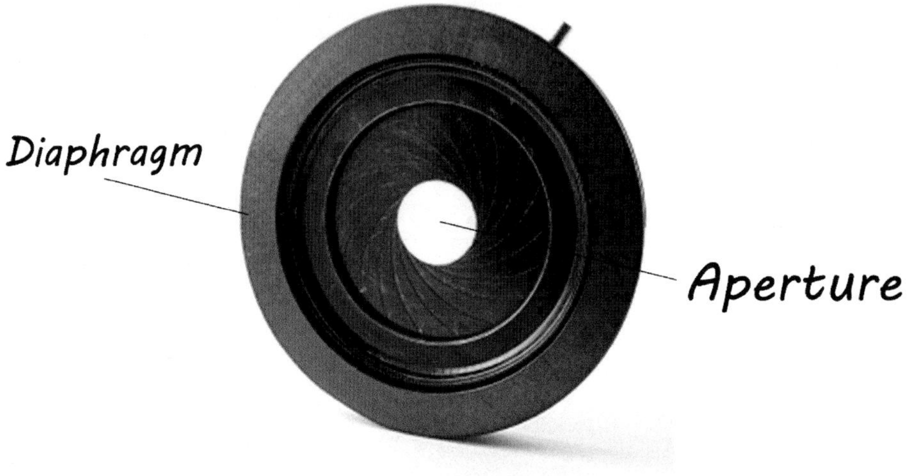

Diaphragm

Aperture

The assembly shown in the photo above is referred to as the **DIAPHRAGM** and is typically mounted between two of the simple lenses that make up the camera **Lens**. The **DIAPHRAGM** is the donut, and the **APERTURE** is the doughnut hole.

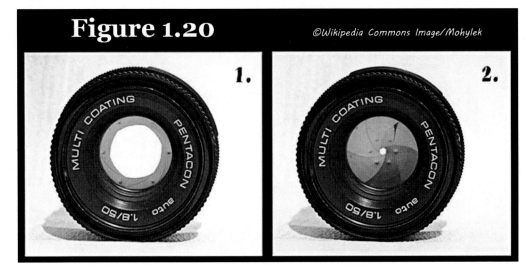

Figure 1.20

(Figure 1.20) shows a large (1) and a small (2) Aperture for the same lens.

What is a Shutter?

A **SHUTTER** is a device that is used to regulate the amount of *time* that the film or SENSOR is exposed to light. Shutters are either open or closed. By regulating the amount of time that a Shutter is open, the photographer controls exposure and some artistic effects that we will discuss in a later chapter.

There are two types of shutters commonly used in cameras – the Leaf Shutter and the Curtain Shutter.

The **LEAF SHUTTER** is a lot like the Aperture Diaphragm, except that it is either totally closed **(Figure 1.21)** or wide open **(Figure 1.22)**. The Leaf Shutter is used in Digital Point-and-Shoot as well as Medium- and Large-Format cameras.

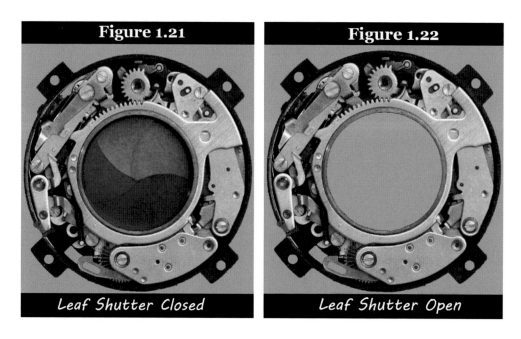

Figure 1.21 — *Leaf Shutter Closed*

Figure 1.22 — *Leaf Shutter Open*

The **CURTAIN SHUTTER (Figure 1.23)** is used in all DSLR Cameras. It has two curtains that move vertically to expose the Sensor to the light coming through the Lens. When using a flash attachment or the Built-in flash device, the timing of the flash can be synchronized to either curtain. The explanation for this feature will be discussed in *Book 2: The Art of Photography*. For now, it is enough to say that the choice of syncing with one shutter or the other is based on artistic considerations.

Figure 1.23

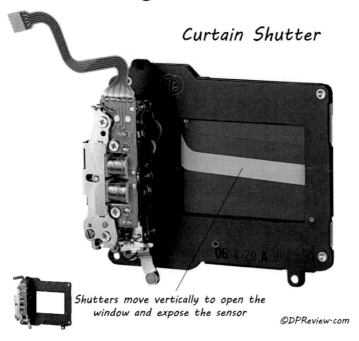

Curtain Shutter

Shutters move vertically to open the
window and expose the sensor

©DPReview·com

As depicted in **(Figure 1.24)**, the shutter is normally closed, preventing light from striking the Sensor.

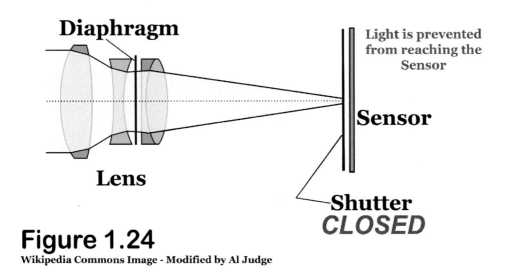

Figure 1.24
Wikipedia Commons Image - Modified by Al Judge

When the Shutter release button is activated on the camera, the shutter opens **(Figure 1.25)** for a pre-determined period of time.

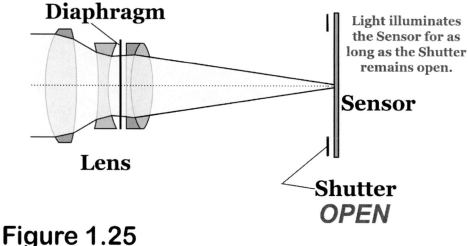

Figure 1.25
Wikipedia Commons Image - Modified by Al Judge

Also note that the light passes through the Aperture (controlled by the Diaphragm based on the photographer's settings) before it gets to the shutter. We will talk more about the relationship of Aperture and Shutter Speed later, but for now, just remember:

The size of the Aperture and the amount of time that the Shutter is open determine the amount of light that strikes the Sensor. This quantity of light is also referred to as the EXPOSURE.

Now, let's put the pieces together to make a camera:

The Digital SLR Camera

The Digital SLR Camera will be discussed in great detail in this book because it should be the camera of choice for anyone who is serious about creating photographs that are more than snapshots. DSLR's also provide a great teaching platform.

If you understand DSLR's, you can easily move to any other camera by simply acquainting yourself with the controls.

A brief inspection of the Owner's Manual will normally be sufficient to get you up and running with a new camera.

Figure 1.26

Digital SLR Camera with 5 Lenses

A key feature of DSLR's is the ability to change lenses **(Figure 1.26)**. We will talk a lot more about **Lenses** later in the book, but for now, just remember:

- If you get serious about photography, you will spend more money on Lenses than Cameras.
- A Lens should be your first upgrade in equipment.
- Unlike Cameras, which depreciate rapidly, Interchangeable Lenses retain their value and are often used for decades on several generations of a camera model.
- When you buy a new digital camera, you can often use your current supply of Lenses. Check compatibility before making a buying decision.
- A surprising number of Lenses that were designed for 35 mm film cameras also work on their Digital counterparts. For example, most Canon Lenses made for Film versions of the Rebel product line, work on the newest Digital Canon Rebel models as well.

Another key feature of DSLR cameras is that the Viewfinder allows you to look *through* the camera Lens when you are composing your images, thus eliminating the need for a separate *viewing* lens. This has not always been the case for cameras, as we will see in **Figure 1.33** – soon to come.

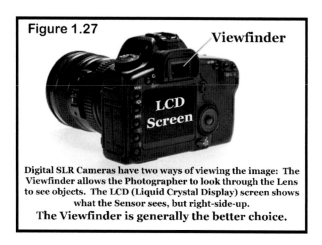

Figure 1.27

Viewfinder

LCD Screen

Digital SLR Cameras have two ways of viewing the image: The Viewfinder allows the Photographer to look through the Lens to see objects. The LCD (Liquid Crystal Display) screen shows what the Sensor sees, but right-side-up.

The Viewfinder is generally the better choice.

The Viewfinder and the LCD Screen **(Figure 1.27)** both have limitations that we will discuss in future chapters. Professionals are partial to the Viewfinder for several reasons that are not critical to our current discussion. Before we are done, you will know how and when to use each method.

Schematic Diagram of a Digital SLR Camera

ALL DSLR Cameras have the following 6 Features

1) A Removable Compound Lens Which Includes the Diaphragm
2) A Movable Mirror - Two positions : 45° or Horizontal
3) A Viewfinder Assembly which Includes a Pentaprism
4) A Curtain Shutter that is normally closed
5) An Electronic Sensor
6) An LCD Screen

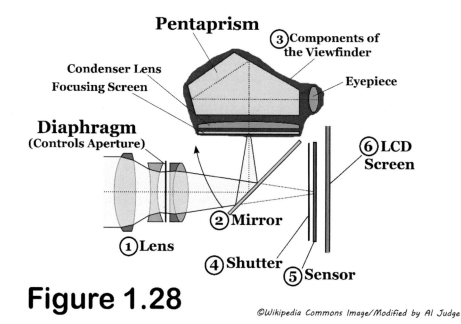

Pentaprism

③ Components of the Viewfinder

Condenser Lens
Focusing Screen

Eyepiece

Diaphragm
(Controls Aperture)

⑥ LCD Screen

② Mirror

① Lens

④ Shutter
⑤ Sensor

Figure 1.28

©Wikipedia Commons Image/Modified by Al Judge

Digital SLRs can be quite overwhelming at first but are easy to master if you understand the individual components and how they work together.

As **Figure 1.28** points out, there are 6 features that are present in every DSLR camera. None of these things is very intimidating by itself, and so we will address them one-by-one.

Each of the points made here will be developed in more detail later in the book.

Referring to **Figure 1.29**, the Lens (1) is removable and contains the **DIAPHRAGM** which controls the size of the Aperture. Most Lenses also allow you to choose between Auto-Focus and Manual Focus. I recommend Manual Focus except for a few specific situations which we will discuss in another chapter. Some Lenses also allow you to select Image Stabilization. This choice should only be done when using the camera hand-held. When we discuss Lenses in Chapter Four, I will explain this feature and how it works.

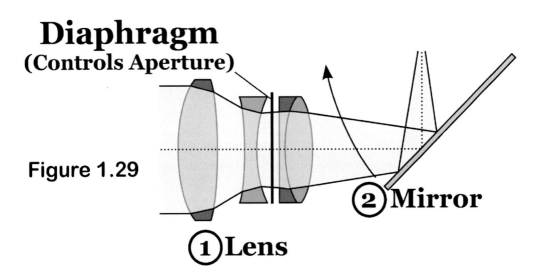

Diaphragm
(Controls Aperture)

Figure 1.29

②**Mirror**

①**Lens**

In (**Figure 1.29**), the image striking the Mirror (2) is an inverted image for the same reason as the image created by the pinhole in **Figure 1.2**.

The *moveable* **MIRROR** is unique to SLR cameras – both film and digital (DSLR) – and is what allows the Photographer to look through the Lens when composing shots. There are several advantages to this, but there are also times when you will want to lock the mirror in the horizontal position. The Mirror can only be in one of two positions – 45° or horizontal. It changes position automatically when the Shutter Button is activated. It can also be manually moved to the horizontal position for cleaning the Sensor and for very fast exposures. We will talk more about these settings a little later in the book.

For now, just remember:

- The Mirror MUST be in the 45° position to use the Viewfinder.
- The Mirror MUST be in the Horizontal position to open the Shutter and capture an image.
- You cannot see anything through the viewfinder when the Shutter is Open and the Mirror is horizontal.
- You cannot take a picture when the Mirror is in the 45° position.

The Viewfinder (3) in **Figure 1.28** and **Figure 1.30** consists of several components including the Pentaprism which flips the inverted image created by the Camera Lens.

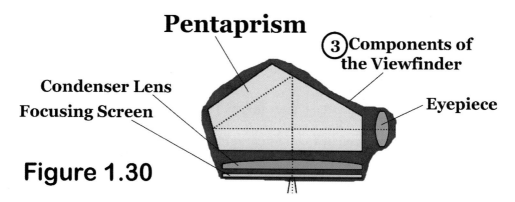

As I mentioned earlier, the Viewfinder is generally the best way to compose your shot. It does not consume any battery power and changes in lighting are instantly observed. For people like me, it has one unfortunate limitation. That limitation will be easier to explain after we have discussed the next two illustrations.

Referring back to Figure 1.28:

We have already talked about the Shutter (4) and Sensor (5) and will go into more detail about these items a bit later. For previewing your shot, the LCD Screen (6) has both advantages and disadvantages when compared to the Viewfinder. We'll return to that topic in a later chapter.

Let's take another look at the schematic first presented in **Figure 1.28**, but this time see what happens when the Shutter is closed (**Figure 1.31**). The Shutter spends most of its time in this position.

SHUTTER CLOSED

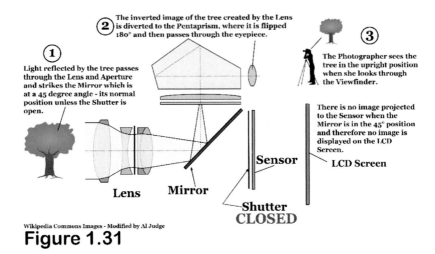

② The inverted image of the tree created by the Lens is diverted to the Pentaprism, where it is flipped 180° and then passes through the eyepiece.

① Light reflected by the tree passes through the Lens and Aperture and strikes the Mirror which is at a 45 degree angle - its normal position unless the Shutter is open.

③ The Photographer sees the tree in the upright position when she looks through the Viewfinder.

There is no image projected to the Sensor when the Mirror is in the 45° position and therefore no image is displayed on the LCD Screen.

Sensor

LCD Screen

Lens   Mirror

Shutter
CLOSED

Wikipedia Commons Images - Modified by Al Judge

Figure 1.31

In this case, the image of the tree passes through the camera Lens and is diverted by the Mirror at a 45° angle to a Pentaprism where it is flipped right-side-up and viewed through the Eyepiece by the photographer. This allows the photographer to see exactly the same thing that the Sensor will see when the Shutter is opened. Thus, the photographer can **FRAME** his or her image. To "FRAME," means to decide exactly how much of the scene in front of the camera will be included in the photo. This view of the scene also aids the photographer in focusing – another topic that we will be addressing in more detail later in the book.

Next, let's take a look at what happens when the shutter opens (**Figure 1.32**) – usually for much less than a second.

SHUTTER OPEN

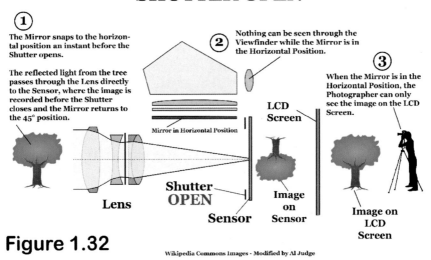

① The Mirror snaps to the horizontal position an instant before the Shutter opens.

The reflected light from the tree passes through the Lens directly to the Sensor, where the image is recorded before the Shutter closes and the Mirror returns to the 45° position.

② Nothing can be seen through the Viewfinder while the Mirror is in the Horizontal Position.

③ When the Mirror is in the Horizontal Position, the Photographer can only see the image on the LCD Screen.

Mirror in Horizontal Position

LCD Screen

Shutter
OPEN

Lens

Sensor

Image on Sensor

Image on LCD Screen

Figure 1.32

Wikipedia Commons Images - Modified by Al Judge

When the Shutter Release Button is pressed, the Mirror automatically flips out of the way to a horizontal position just before the shutter opens. In this case, the image of the tree is projected onto the Sensor where it is recorded in an inverted position. At a pre-determined time, the shutter closes and the mirror snaps back into place. Nothing is visible through the eyepiece when the mirror flips up to expose the Shutter and Sensor. There are times when you will want to lock the mirror in the horizontal position. We will talk about that later in the book.

The noise that we associate with snapping pictures is mostly the result of the mirror movement. The Shutter also makes some noise but is much quieter than the mirror.

Now, back to my earlier comment about a Viewfinder limitation. Viewfinders have a "Diopter Correction" knob somewhere near where you place your eye. This allows you to fine-tune the Viewfinder for your eyes and often allows people who wear glasses to look through the Viewfinder without their glasses. For me, the "Diopter Correction" doesn't quite do it and I can't see very well through the Viewfinder even with my glasses. This was a dilemma for me until I started using the LCD Screen to put the final touch on Manual Focusing.

Using the Viewfinder, I compose my shot and focus as well as I can. I then switch to "Live View" which moves the Mirror to the Horizontal Position and opens the shutter so that the image is shown on the LCD. I then select a spot in the image where I want to focus and magnify that spot by a factor of 10. I complete the manual focusing and return to normal viewing through the viewfinder. I could take a shot in "Live View" but this mode uses a lot of power and causes the Sensor to heat up which can cause "Noise" or graininess in the photo. In many cases, I can compose and capture several shots before I have to focus again. This is particularly effective in landscape photography.

Not all DSLR cameras have a "Live View" function or its equivalent. We will talk more about that in the next chapter.

©iStockphoto·com/AK2

Twin Lens Reflex Camera (TLR)

Figure 1.33

The SLR camera got its name from the way that it deflects the light to the eyepiece. The word Reflex means Reflected Light.

Some Medium- **(Figure 1.33)** and Large-Format cameras have two lenses – one for viewing and composing the scene and the other for capturing the image. They are called TLRs – **Twin** Lens Reflex cameras. The Mirror is permanently mounted at a 45° angle in these cameras. When the camera is close to the subject, there can be a noticeable difference between the image on the viewfinder and the image recorded.

Thus, the name, **Single Lens Reflex** or **SLR**, identifies a camera where the image passes through a *single* lens and is *reflected* by a mirror to the eyepiece right-side-up by the Pentaprism.

If we take another look at **Figure 1.8** from earlier in the chapter, the cut-away of the 35 mm camera should look more familiar and less intimidating now that we have dissected it.

35 mm SLR Film Camera Cut-Away

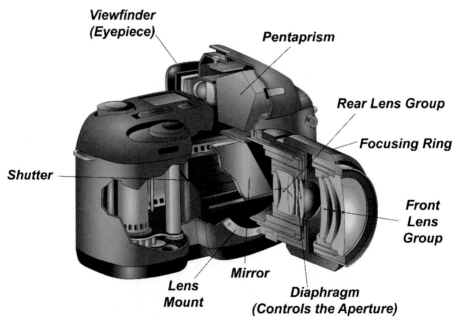

Figure 1.34

Wikipedia Commons Image/ Anuskafm
Modified by Al Judge

A Digital SLR is identical except for the fact that the film is replaced by the Sensor and an LCD Screen has been added to the back of the camera.

Remember that our detailed discussion has been in relation to SLR cameras. Point-and-Shoot cameras don't have interchangeable Lenses, Optical Viewfinders, Pentaprisms, or Mirrors to reflect the image. Large-Format Cameras do not have Viewfinders or Mirrors. Medium-Format cameras can be like DSLRs or Large-Format cameras.

Some Things to Remember

The primary difference between a film camera and a digital camera is that in digital cameras the image is recorded by a photosensitive **SENSOR** rather than film. The digital image files created by the Sensor are stored on memory cards.

SENSOR SIZE and **LENS** QUALITY are the two most important factors affecting image quality.

Sensors in **DSLR** cameras are 20 to 40 times the size of sensors in entry-level point-and-shoot cameras.

A camera **LENS** is actually a collection of simple lenses with a common axis that work together to create a sharp image. Another term for this type of Lens is **COMPOUND LENS**.

In this book, a compound lens is assumed when **LENS** is mentioned. In photographic terms, this is the meaning of the term **LENS**.

Some important characteristics of a **LENS** are **FOCAL LENGTH** and **VIEW ANGLE**.

The size of the **APERTURE** and the amount of *time* that the **SHUTTER** is open determine the amount of light that strikes the Sensor. This *Quantity of Light* is called the *Exposure*.

If you get serious about photography, you will spend more money on Lenses than Cameras.

A Lens should be your first upgrade in equipment.

Unlike Cameras, Lenses retain their value and are often used for decades.

When you buy a new camera, you can often use your current supply of Lenses.

Single Lens Reflex or **SLR**, identifies a camera in which the image passes through a *single lens* and is *reflected* by a mirror to the eyepiece right-side-up by the Pentaprism.

Photographic Terms Introduced in this Chapter

Digital Camera   A camera in which the image is recorded by a photosensitive electronic SENSOR.

Film Camera   A camera in which the image is recorded on photographic film.

Frame (noun)   A portion of a roll of film that contains one image.

Negative   A photographic master print from which Positive (Normal) Prints are made. The tonal values are the exact opposite of the Positive or Print. In other words, white appears as black on the negative and black appears as white. Negatives can be glass plates, photographic film, or digital files.

Darkroom   A dedicated light-proof room in which film negatives and prints are processed in trays of chemical solutions. During the process, the only light in the room is a dim red bulb.

Contact Prints   A process by which photographic negatives are placed in physical contact with light-sensitive photo paper and exposed to a burst of light. The photo paper is then treated in trays of chemicals in order to develop the image.

SLR (Single Lens Reflex) Camera   A particular style of camera that allows the photographer to look through the lens in order to compose his image. It contains a moveable mirror to deflect the image to the viewfinder and a Pentaprism to flip it right-side-up. SLRs also use removable lenses.

Medium-Format Camera   A camera that captures an image on film or digital sensor that is larger than 2.25 in. X 2.25 in. but less than 4in X 5 in

Large-Format Camera   A camera that captures an image on film or digital sensor that is 4-inch X 5-inch or larger.

Digital SLR – DSLR   An SLR Camera in which the image is recorded by an electronic Sensor.

Sensor   An electronic device which captures and records photons of light and translates color and quantity of light data to Pixels that then form an image.

Pixel   A PIcture ELement or point of measureable color intensity and tone that is one element of a Mosaic-like image composed of many such elements – often in the millions.

Photosite   A specific location on a photographic sensor where photons of a particular color of light are collected, counted, and recorded.

Simple Lens   A single piece of glass or plastic that refracts (bends) light in such a way that it converges to a point or diverges in a diffuse manner.

Focal Point   A point at which the light passing through a lens converges.

Focal Length   The distance from the midplane of a lens to the focal point of the same lens. Usually measured in millimeters (mm).

Focal Plane   A Plane parallel to the midplane of a lens, also containing the Focal Point. Photographic film and Sensors are located in this plane.

View Angle   The angular expanse of the area visible through the viewfinder for a particular lens. It can be measured horizontally, vertically, or diagonally.

Aberration   A deviation from the norm, or a defect in the characteristics of a lens.

Compound Lens   A collection of simple lenses that share a common axis in order to improve and focus the image passing through the Lens and onto the film or Sensor. The type of Lens assembly implied when a Photographer refers to his or her Lens.

Pentaprism   A special type of lens that is unique to SLR Cameras, and whose only purpose is to flip the image coming through the lens so that it can be observed right-side-up through the Viewfinder.

Aperture   The opening in the Diaphragm of a Compound Lens through which the image must pass. A means of blocking unwanted light from reaching the Sensor. A hole through which light travels.

Diaphragm   A device made up of several moveable blades that move in tandem to form and size the Aperture. It functions very much like the Iris of the human eye. It is usually sandwiched between two of the simple lenses that form a compound lens.

Shutter   A device whose purpose is to block light from the photographic recording medium except when an image is being captured. It opens and closes like the blink of an eye. It can also be held open for long periods of time in low-light situations.

Leaf Shutter   A type of shutter used in digital Point-and-Shoot cameras as well as Medium- and Large-Format cameras. It operates very much like the Diaphragm but is either wide open or totally closed.

Curtain Shutter   The type of Shutter used in SLR cameras – both film and digital. Two horizontal curtains that move vertically to expose the sensor or film.

Viewfinder   A device that allows the photographer to view and compose his image.

LCD (Liquid Crystal Display) Screen   A small electronic display panel on the back of digital cameras used to display camera settings and review images.

Mirror   A mirror which is normally in a 45° position in order to deflect the image coming through the camera lens to the Viewfinder. It snaps to a horizontal position just before the shutter opens and returns to its normal position just after the shutter closes. It can also be manually moved to the horizontal position for cleaning the Sensor, Live View, and very fast exposures.

Frame (verb)   To limit the amount of the scene that will be captured by the camera. A step in composing an image.

Chapter Two – Before you Buy a Camera ...

Before we talk about your options in the world of Digital Cameras, there are a few things that we need to discuss briefly.

As we mentioned in Chapter One, Lens Quality and Sensor Size are the two most important factors regarding image quality.

For now, all you need to know about Lenses is that the ability to change Lenses is a big deal and highly desirable. We will talk about Lenses in detail in Chapter Four.

So, let's move on to Sensors.

Digital Camera Sensors

There are two types of Sensors used in Digital Cameras – CMOS and CCD. CMOS dominates the market, but most manufacturers offer at least one model with a CCD Sensor. In 2012, Canon had only one Camera Model that used a CCD Sensor and 33 that used a CMOS Sensor. Nikon, on the other hand, had 13 CCD Models and 18 CMOS Models.

CCD (Charge Coupled Device) Sensors are commonly used in precision digital imaging applications for science and medicine. It is generally accepted that they produce the highest quality image. They are also more expensive to produce, use more power, and run hotter than CMOS Sensors. Because of the heat that they produce, they are susceptible to creating a grainy effect in the image. In very expensive scientific and medical equipment, the heat can be dissipated to reduce or eliminate this problem.

CMOS (Complementary Metal-Oxide-Semiconductor) Sensors are known for their low power consumption. This means more photos on a battery charge and less electrical "Noise" which can cause a grainy effect in photos. The images produced by CMOS Sensors have improved greatly in the last decade and are quite good. Because of the grainy effect of CCD Sensors, not everyone agrees that they produce significantly better images *in digital cameras* than the current generation of CMOS Sensors.

Both devices get their names from the manufacturing processes that produce them.

Once again, ***Sensor Size*** should be your biggest concern.

The following chart gives some perspective as well as specific values for some of the more popular Sensors. What counts is the *AREA* of the Sensor, which is listed in Millimeters Squared.

As you can see in **Figure 2.1**, the Sensor in Digital Point-and-Shoot Cameras is a really tiny device. A Full-Frame Sensor is almost 32 times as large.

Popular Digital Camera Sensor Sizes

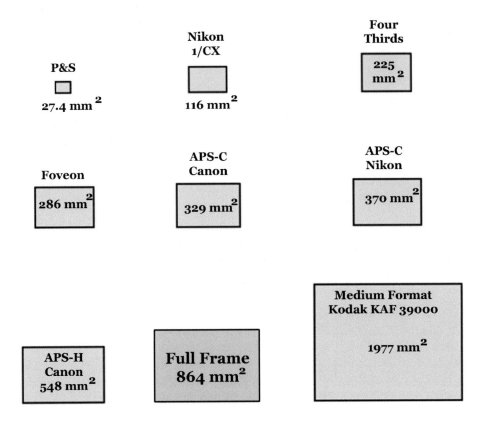

Figure 2.1

The next three sizes – Nikon 1/CX, Four Thirds, and Foveon – are used in "Bridge" Cameras, also called Compact Cameras. These Cameras "Bridge the Gap" between Point-and-Shoot Cameras and DSLRs.

The Sensors with the APS designation are called Cropped-Frame Sensors and are used in DSLR Cameras. They are called Cropped because they are smaller than the Full-Frame Sensor. The APS designation is another carryover from film photography. **APS stands for Advanced Photo System**. It was a new type of film introduced by several camera manufacturers in 1996. It never really took off for a variety of reasons and was rapidly rendered obsolete by digital cameras. It was discontinued by various manufacturers between 2004 and 2011. **APS-H** is "High Definition" and **APS-C** is "Classic." These designations are used as a way of conveying size. An APS-C Sensor is "roughly" the size of a frame of APS-C film.

The Full-Frame Sensor is the Digital equivalent to a frame of 35 mm film. Its actual dimensions are 36 mm X 24 mm. It is the standard of measurement for DSLR Cameras.

As you can also see in **Figure 2.1**, a Medium-Format Sensor can be quite a bit larger than a DSLR Camera's Sensor.

We will discuss the various categories of Digital Cameras in the next chapter, but a little further background might be helpful here.

In addition to the Sensor, every digital camera has some type of "**IMAGING CORE.**" This is like the CPU of a computer. It not only processes and saves the images recorded on the Sensor, but it controls color, autofocus, auto exposure, and a wide variety of other functions. Canon's name for this device is **DIGIC** (**DIG**ital **I**maging **C**ore) and Nikon calls it **EXPEED**. Current Versions are Digic 5+ and Expeed 3. In general, the higher the number the newer and more powerful the processor. Every Camera maker will have its own version of this processor. I mentioned Canon and Nikon because they dominate the market.

You really don't need to worry about this very much. I just want you to be familiar with these terms since they will be part of the camera specs. For example, the description might say "Full-Frame CMOS, Digic5+." This brief chapter should take the mystery out of that statement.

Earlier in the book, I said that Megapixels is not the way to judge a camera. But now that you have an idea of how much Sensor Size varies, I will also tell you that:

For a given Sensor Size, the more Pixels the better.

There are a few other factors in the Sensor design and Imaging Core design that affect overall image quality, but they are related to more advanced topics that are beyond the scope of this book.

File Formats

There are currently two formats used for saving the camera's digital images – **RAW** and **Jpeg**.

The RAW format simply means that the image file saved by the camera contains every detail of image data that the camera is capable of capturing. RAW files cannot be altered in any way. They can, however, be processed by special software and then saved in a different file format.

RAW is the preferred format of professionals and should be used by anyone who is serious about photography.

We will talk about this in more detail later in the book.

You may already be familiar with the Jpeg format since this is the standard format for sending images over the Internet. Jpeg (Joint Photographic Experts

Group) is a standard that was created to make it easier and faster to display images on Web pages and to send image files over the Internet. Most people can't tell the difference between a Jpeg and a RAW file image created from the same number of pixels, but your ability to edit and enhance your images will be greatly compromised by the Jpeg format since it discards image data.

If you choose a Jpeg format for storing your images, your camera's imaging-core processor will start discarding pixel data according to a Jpeg algorithm (a step-by-step procedure for calculating what to toss and what to keep). Depending on the type of Digital camera, you may have several choices in file size and compression. My camera's Jpeg size options are Small, Medium, and Large. My compression options are Normal and Fine. The Fine setting will be a larger file containing more detail.

Image **Compression** is also an algorithm that discards image data. Because of the Jpeg format and compression, most of the image data can be discarded and still produce a nice image on a computer screen. Jpeg files are often referred to as "lossy" because they discard or lose so much data.

For my camera, a RAW or Large Jpeg file will be based on 15.1 Megapixels of data. If I choose a Medium Jpeg, the file will be based on 8 Megapixels of image data. If I choose a Small Jpeg, the file will be based on 3.7 Megapixels of image data. The Sensor records the same information for all these situations, but the camera discards a portion of it for the smaller file options.

Many people incorrectly equate Megapixels with Megabytes and assume that a 16 MP camera will produce image files that are 16 MB in size. This is not correct.

There is no simple formula for calculating the actual file size for each option. I did an exercise to demonstrate this point.

I took three shots of exactly the same thing about 30 seconds apart. I made no adjustments and did not move the camera. The lighting was changing rapidly due to cloud cover from a winter storm. The RAW files for these three shots were 20.1 MB, 18.89 MB, and 17.89 MB – a variation of more than 10% for the exact same image. The only difference was the lighting due to cloud coverage. A brighter image will generally result in a larger file with more detail.

I then took a series of photos of the *exact same scene* with the six Jpeg options that I have on my camera.

A Large Image based on 15.1 Megapixels resulted in
6.71 MB Fine
3.15 MB Normal

A Medium Image based on 8 Megapixels resulted in
3.73 MB Fine
1.71 MB Normal

A Small Image based on 3.7 Megapixels resulted in
1.92 MB Fine
0.85 MB Normal

As you can see in **Figure 2.2**, Jpeg files can be significantly smaller than RAW files. Jpegs also vary greatly based on the selected image quality.

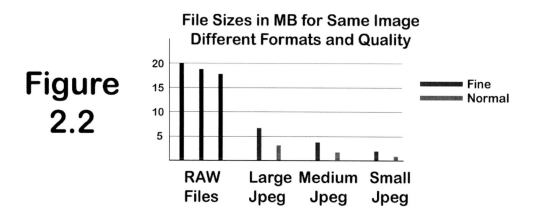

Some Things to Remember

CMOS Sensors dominate the Digital SLR market.

Sensor Size is far more important than the number of pixels.

For a given Sensor size, the more pixels the better.

A Full-Frame Sensor is nearly 32 times the size of a Point-and-Shoot Sensor.

RAW is the preferred format of professionals and should be used by anyone who is serious about photography.

Photographic Terms Introduced in this Chapter

CCD (Charge Coupled Device)   Sensors commonly used in precision digital imaging applications for science and medicine. Less common in digital cameras.

CMOS (Complementary Metal-Oxide-Semiconductor)   The type of Sensor that dominates the Digital camera market.

APS (Advanced Photo System)   An obsolete 1996 Standard for higher quality camera film. It never caught on for a variety of reasons including the success of digital cameras.

APS-H Sensor   A Sensor roughly the size of a frame of APS High-Defintion film.

APS-C Sensor   A Sensor roughly the size of a frame of APS Classic film.

IMAGING CORE   The Digital Camera equivalent of a computer's CPU.

DIGIC (DIGital Imaging Core)   Canon's Imaging Core Processor.

EXPEED   Nikon's Imaging Core Processor.

RAW   A file format for photographic images that saves ALL the image data that the camera is capable of recording.

Jpeg (Joint Photographic Experts Group)   A file format for photographic images that creates compressed files for easy and rapid transmission over the Internet and on Webpages.

File Compression   A process for reducing the file size while maintaining critical data.

Chapter Three – Your Digital Camera Choices

In this chapter, we will explore the types of digital cameras that are currently available. We will review each type of camera first and then compare features, price, and limitations across categories. All prices quoted will be for Amazon.com. This is not for the purpose of promoting Amazon.com, but for the sake of comparative pricing.

****

Before we proceed, it might be helpful to add some perspective to our task at hand. We will be discussing five categories of digital cameras. The brief description for each is just a highlight of what to expect in this chapter.

Each category will be more expensive and offer more features than the previous category, except for the second category – Compact Cameras. The categories are:

Point-and-Shoot   Small, compact, under $200, Lens is Built-in, image files are saved in Jpeg Format only.

Compact (Bridge Cameras)   More Features than Point-and-Shoot but fewer than DSLR. Cost can be as much as DSLR. Not easily summarized because of diversity of features and price.

DSLR (Digital Single Lens Reflex)   This is the camera of choice for most professionals and serious photographers. It is also the standard by which we will measure all other cameras. Extremely versatile. There is no Lens built into the camera. It uses Interchangeable Lenses that allow the photographer to select a Lens that optimizes her images. Image files can be saved in RAW format as well as Jpeg.

Medium-Format   Normally system cameras – assembled from components to provide a camera that closely fits the photographer's needs. Produce images that are considerably larger than DSLR images. Very expensive. Typically, $20,000 to $50,000.

Large-Format   Highest Quality Images. Can be quite large. Easily recognized by light-tight collapsible bellows. Film versions still dominate this segment. Very expensive and built from components, much like Medium-Format Cameras.

****

Point–and–Shoot (P&S)

I chose this camera at random from the Amazon.com website. As I am writing this, the current price is $119. This is typical for this class of camera.

Timer Warning and Redeye Flash

On / Off Button

Flash

Shutter Button

Microphone

Adjust View - Telephoto / Wide Angle

Telescoping Lens

Figure 3.1   Nikon P&S

I don't own this camera and have never used this model of camera, so if you are reading this and discover a mistake, please send me (ajudex@hotmail.com) an email with "Book Error" in the Subject Line.

Most camera features are standardized and use the same symbols, so even though I have never used this particular camera, I should know how to operate it by just glancing over the buttons. Let's go clockwise around the camera starting on the left.

The **Adjust View** ring is concentric with the Shutter Button and rotates a few degrees left and right. It helps you to frame the scene by zooming in and out. There is a small projection on the front of the ring. There is a "W" printed on the camera on one side of the ring. If you push the projection toward the "W" it will be like walking backward when you look at the image on the back of the camera. This is the Wide-Angle View. On the opposite side of the knob, there is a "T" for Telephoto. If you push the projection in this direction, you will zoom in on the scene.

You press down on the **Shutter Button** to take a picture or start the timer.

The **Timer Warning / Red Eye Flash Light** has two functions. (1) If you set the timer and press the Shutter button, it will begin blinking. After a few seconds – usually 2 seconds or 10 seconds – the camera will activate the shutter and take a picture. At the very last second, the light will send out a small flash. This flash helps to reduce Red Eye in your photos. (2) Any time that you use the flash, this light will also flash first to reduce Red Eye even if people aren't your subject.

The **On/Off Button** is a sure thing since it is printed on the camera next to the button. I see a small ring around the button. This ring will be lit when the camera is turned on.

The **Flash** is a small light that will flash in certain modes – a topic that we will cover when we get to the back of the camera.

The **Microphone** is located behind the two small holes at the top of the lens – one on each side of the Lens. If you shoot video be sure to keep your fingers away from this area.

This particular camera has a **Telescoping Lens**. This is not always the case. The telescoping lens provides a wider range of zoom capability.

Let's go clockwise around the back of the camera **(Figure 3.2)** starting on the left again.

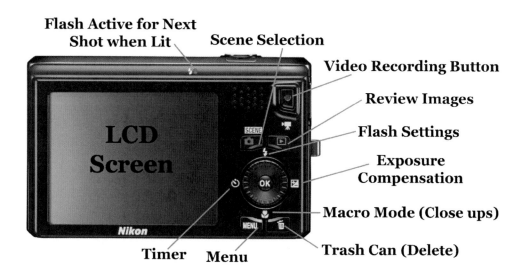

Figure 3.2   Nikon P&S

There is a small light above the LCD Screen that will be lit in certain camera modes. This is to let you know that the flash will fire. It has a small bolt-of-lightning icon next to it. I have designated it as **Flash Active**.

Scene Selection This button lets you choose from several preset conditions or modes. The number of choices is increasing daily, but some of the more universal modes are:

- **Portrait** Use when taking pictures of people and animals or whenever you want your subject to stand out against a blurred background.
- **Landscape** Use for landscape shots or anytime that your subject is far away. It will keep the focus sharp for most or all of the picture.

- **Sports** Use this mode to freeze the action of a sports event or similar situation.
- **Kids & Pets** This is a hybrid of the Portrait and Sports modes. It is a Portrait that takes into consideration the fact that kids and pets are rarely still.
- **Night Mode/ Night Portrait** This will adjust the brightness of the scene so that you can see the faces of people in a photo that is taken at night.
- **Fireworks** Camera settings are optimized for this situation.
- **Beach and Snow** This will darken the image enough that you can make out details in these very bright situations.

Video Recording Button Usually press to start the video recording, then press again to stop the recording.

Review Images When you press this button, the last photo that you took will be displayed on the LCD Screen. To go backwards through your images, press the large ring below it on the left side next to the Timer Icon. To go forward, press the ring on the right side next to the Exposure Compensation Icon. If you are at your last photo and press the right side, it will display your first photo. It is a continuous loop of images. When viewing images, the normal functions of the ring are overridden so that it can serve two purposes. Press the Review Images Button a second time to close the images and return to normal functions.

Flash Settings Press the ring near this icon to make adjustments to the intensity of the flash. Sometimes this function will also let you tell the camera if you don't want to use the flash, but this is not always the case.

Exposure Compensation If your pictures appear too bright or too dark on the screen, you can press the ring near here to make adjustments. Unfortunately, LCD screens don't always accurately display the image and you might discover that your pictures look much different on your computer monitor. Ultimately, you might have to learn the proper setting by trial and error.

Macro Mode This is the close-up mode. It is for getting very close to small objects. Bugs and flowers are the most likely subjects, but it works well with coins and other small objects as well.

Trash Can (Delete) When you are reviewing photos, this button is used to delete the throwaways (yes, we all take them from time to time!). It is also the cancel button for making Menu changes.

Menu This is the button for setting the clock and date on your camera and several preferences. The exact Menu items will depend on the specific model of camera, so I don't have a clue what is included in the menu for this particular camera. Menu items are usually intuitive and simple to set.

Timer This selection allows you to take pictures of yourself or join in a group photo. You would make a timer selection by pressing the ring next to the icon. Most cameras give you at least two time periods to choose from. Two seconds and 10 seconds are the most common choices. After making your choice, position the camera on a flat surface, press the Shutter Button, and run for your spot in the scene.

Benefits of P&S (Point-and-Shoot) Cameras

- Inexpensive – Usually below $200.
- Small – Can easily fit into a pocket or purse.
- Requires minimal learning curve.
- Numerous preset modes.
- Takes pretty good **Snapshots**.

Drawbacks of P&S Cameras

- Photographer has no control over the results other than holding the camera steady and pointing it in the right direction.
- A very small Sensor results in fair quality images, even with a lot of mexapixels.
- There is no optical Viewfinder.
- The camera MUST be held away from the body in order to see the image on the LCD Screen. This makes "Camera Shake" much more likely.
- The LCD Screen can be hard to see in bright daylight.
- Image files can only be saved in Jpeg Format. We will talk more about this later in the book.
- Lens is built-in and cannot be changed.

Additional Perspectives on P&S Cameras

This category of Digital Cameras includes iPhones, iPads, and any other Smartphone or portable device with a built-in Camera. As a result, sales for Point-and-Shoot cameras are declining. A large percentage of the population carries a Smartphone with them at all times and the quality of the photos taken with Cell Phones has improved dramatically over the last few years.

Compact Cameras

This is a relatively new category of camera and can be a bit confusing because of a lack of consistency in terminology. For example, some manufacturers use the term **Compact** to refer to smaller and less expensive Point-and-Shoot cameras. Other terms that are helpful in finding this category of camera are **Bridge Camera** and **Compact System Camera**.

Bridge Cameras are cameras with more features and capabilities than Point-and-Shoot cameras but less capability than DSLR cameras.

System Cameras are cameras that have changeable parts. This general heading includes Medium-Format and Large-Format Cameras. If we add the word Compact before System – Compact System Cameras – we narrow the field to Bridge Cameras that have interchangeable Lenses and other accessory attachments.

When you see the term **Compact Camera,** be aware that it may or may not mean the cameras described in this section. Bridge Cameras and Compact System Cameras are more accurate terms but are not universally used to describe this type of camera.

We will be looking at four different design approaches to a **Compact Camera** in this chapter.

Nikon Coolpix P510

To minimize confusion, let's start with Bridge Cameras with Fixed Lenses. The Nikon Coolpix P510 (**Figure 3.3**) is a great example of this type of digital camera.

Many of the controls and functions are like the P&S camera that we just reviewed, so I won't go over every item – only the ones that constitute an upgrade from P&S cameras. The current price is $ 347.

Figure 3.3   Coolpix P510

This is one of several cameras that I own. One of the reasons that I bought it was for the built-in **GPS** function. This function uses some power, so it is not always on. You must turn it on and off via the menu. A particularly nice feature to this is that you can create a GPS log while you are shooting.

Using the camera's menu, you select a time frame for the log, i.e., 6 hours. The camera's GPS will take readings at regular intervals and enter those readings into the log whether you are taking pictures or not. Nikon does not disclose how often entries are made to the log, but it is frequent enough to pinpoint your location for any picture taken during that period of time. The log will continue until the time period expires or you manually turn it off.

You can then download the GPS log to **Photoshop Lightroom** (a Photo Editing Program) or a similar program and it will add the GPS data to any images in its database that were taken during the time period covered by the log. The great thing about this is that if you use more than one camera during that time frame, the GPS data will be added to all photos that you took. This is possible because Digital Cameras typically imbed date and time information into each image file. So, the camera knows when you took the photo, and the GPS log knows where you were at that time.

A couple of years ago, I took an interesting photo of some tree roots, but it was not as sharp as I would have liked. I went back to take another picture, but it was not where I thought it was. I still have never found the tree. With GPS data it would have been very easy to find.

Referring to **Figure 3.3**, we see that there are two places on the camera where you can adjust the Wide-Angle / Telephoto Zoom. There is also a button that activates a Pop-up built-in Flash.

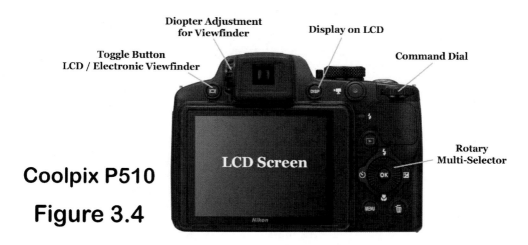

Looking at the back of the camera **(Figure 3.4)** and going left to right and clockwise, the first item is a toggle switch. This button determines whether the image will appear on the LCD Screen or the Electronic Viewfinder. In both cases, the image is created by the sensor.

Although not as desirable as an Optical Viewfinder, the Electronic Viewfinder allows you to hold the camera against your face and view the scene without the glare of the sun or other distractions. This position is much less prone to camera shake than holding the camera in front of you so that you can see the LCD screen. The viewfinder also gives you more freedom for framing your shot.

To the left of the viewfinder is a Diopter Adjustment which allows you to customize the Viewfinder for your eyes.

The Display Button to the right of the Viewfinder allows you to change how much information about your camera settings is displayed on the LCD Screen. There are three levels to choose. The most comprehensive choice lists all your settings around the edges of the image. The second option adds an outline of the exact frame for your image. The third option only tells you the status of your battery.

The **command dial** and **rotary multi-selector** (**Figures 3.4 and 3.5**) allow you to quickly set certain adjustments. For example, in the Manual Mode, the Command Dial sets Shutter Speed and the Rotary Dial sets Aperture Size.

Coolpix P510

Mode Selector

Command Dial

Figure 3.5

The Mode Selector is another major upgrade from P&S cameras.

Figure 3.6

Coolpix
P510

Moving clockwise around the left side of the Selector (**Figure 3.6**):

P = Programmed   The camera selects Aperture and Shutter Speed which you can fine-tune.
S = Shutter   You set the Shutter Speed and the Camera chooses the Aperture
A = Aperture   You set the Aperture and the Camera chooses Shutter Speed.
M = Manual Mode   You choose all the settings.

Moving up to the top:

U = You Setup and save frequently used settings.

Moving on to **Figure 3.7**, and going Counterclockwise around the bottom of the selector:

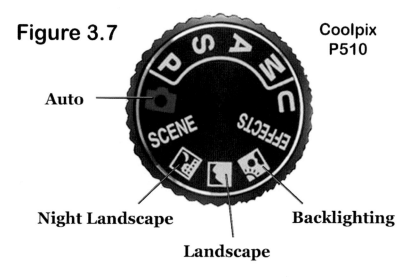

Figure 3.7

Coolpix
P510

Auto

Night Landscape

Landscape

Backlighting

Auto   The Camera makes all decisions. This is a basic P&S option.

Night Landscape   The settings are optimized for situations like a cityscape where you have bright lights and dark skies.

Landscape   Settings are optimized for landscape shots. Sharp focus with more emphasis on blue and green.

Backlighting   Increased exposure is used to illuminate faces when the background is very bright, and faces are in shadows.

SCENE When this option is selected, the **MENU** button will bring up a list of special scenes or situations. You then choose the one that best fits your situation. Your options are:

Portrait	Sports	Night Portrait
Party/Indoors	Beach	Snow
Sunset	Dusk/Dawn	Close-up
Food	Museum	Fireworks
Black & White Copy	Panorama	Pet Portrait

Press OK on the Rotary Multi-Selector (**Figure 3.4**) to make your choice.

Figure 3.8

Coolpix
P510

EFFECTS This option **(Figure 3.8)** adds a special effect to your photo when you take it. Your options are:

Soft	Nostalgic Sepia	High-Contrast Mononchrome
High Key	Low Key	Selective Color
Painting	High-ISO Monochrome	Silhouette

Note: A ***High Key*** image is very bright but not totally overexposed. It will often have a white background. A ***Low Key*** image is very dark, almost black, with only a portion of the subject in the light. Both techniques are used to create drama in the image.

My best advice for learning to apply the Effects is to just experiment with these settings and see what you like.

Another nice feature of this camera is the articulating LCD Screen **(Figure 3.9)**. This makes it easy to hold the camera low to the ground, above your head, or any other unusual position and still see the screen.

Images are stored in Jpeg only. There are 27 combinations of image Size and Quality to choose from.

Figure 3.9   Coolpix P510

This camera also illustrates a very important thing to remember when you buy a camera. Camera manufacturers often make it difficult to find the Sensor data. When I bought this camera, I assumed some things about the Sensor based on all the features and the price. I was very wrong. This particular camera uses the tiny Point-and-Shoot camera Sensor. Fortunately, I only use this camera to scout potential photo shoots. It is small and light and has an impressive telephoto range. I can hike a trail and take snapshots of scenes that I find interesting. Later, I return to those locations with all my gear and a good idea of how I want to capture each image.

Because of the small Point-and-Shoot Sensor, I would not recommend this camera for any other use than snapshots and planning. Otherwise, it is a pretty good compact camera.

Canon G10

So, let's look at another Compact camera, but this time with a larger Sensor. The Canon G10 **(Figures 3.10 and 3.11)** sells for about $800 and has a Sensor that is only slightly larger than the Nikon Coolpix P510 – 43 mm² vs 27 mm².

I won't break it down by features but just point out a few things that attract people to this camera. It is compact and has a fixed lens with a wide range of capabilities. Adapter Lenses can be screwed to the front of the lens to further enhance its capabilities.

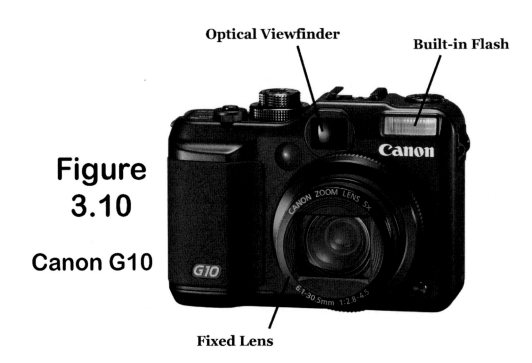

Optical Viewfinder

Built-in Flash

Figure 3.10

Canon G10

Fixed Lens

This camera has a built-in flash as well as a "Hotshoe" for attaching an auxiliary flash. It has an Optical Viewfinder, but the view is through the camera rather than through the lens like a DSLR. For this reason, the viewfinder will not accurately display the image frame. The closer the camera is to the object being photographed, the greater the discrepancy.

Optical Viewfinder

Hotshoe for Flash Attachment

Figure 3.11

Canon G10

Another feature is the ability to save images in RAW as well as Jpeg.

Olympus Pen E-PL1

There is a third type of camera in this general category. It is a compact camera with changeable lenses. Several manufacturers offer cameras of this type. The Olympus Pen E-PL1 **(Figures 3.12 and 3.13)** looks interesting at about $350.

Hotshoe for Attachments

Figure 3.12

Olympus Pen E-PL1

Changeable Lens

There is an optional Electronic Viewfinder that can be attached to the camera through the Hotshoe. The biggest advantage for this camera is a Four Thirds Sensor (See **Figure 2.1** – this is a manufacturer designation, and the Four Thirds name has no significance for our discussion) which is more than 8 times the size of a typical P&S camera Sensor.

Figure 3.13

Canon EOS M

Another option in the compact category is **MIRRORLESS** cameras. There are currently models available from several manufacturers. In Chapter One, we talked a lot about the mirror in a DSLR camera and why it is so important.

Well there are some advantages to eliminating it – mostly size and a wide view-angle – and so some high-end compact cameras have this mirrorless design.

The Canon EOS M **(Figures 3.14 and 3.15)** has an APS-C Sensor which is more than 13 times the size of a P&S camera Sensor. It also has most of the features of a DSLR camera. The most notable drawback is the lack of an optical Viewfinder. This particular model sells for $680 at this time. This type of camera is also known as EVIL – Electronic Viewfinder Interchangeable Lens. There are only two Lenses available for this camera at this time.

Figure 3.14

Canon EOS M

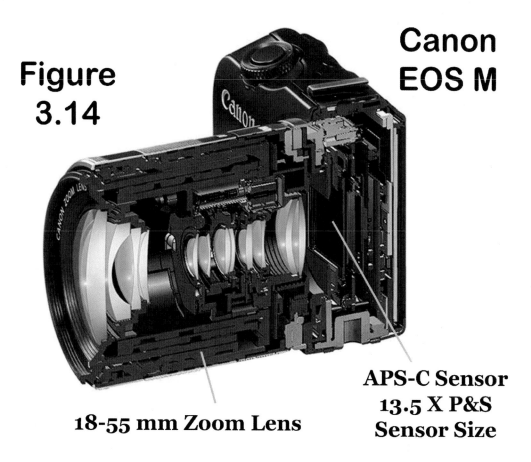

18-55 mm Zoom Lens

**APS-C Sensor
13.5 X P&S
Sensor Size**

I found this image on numerous websites, but none of them attributed the source. I can only
assume that it was part of a Canon Press Release. I (AI Judge) added the notes.

Canon EOS M

Figure 3.15

The following chart summarizes the four types of **Compact Cameras** covered in this Chapter. There may be more by the time this is published. This is a category in transition.

Brand	Model	Sensor Size mm^2	File Formats	Change Lenses	Price
Nikon	Coolpix P510	27	Jpeg	No	$347
Canon	G10	43	Jpeg & RAW	No	$800
Olympus	E-PL1	225	Jpeg	Yes	$350
Canon	EOS M	329	Jpeg & RAW	Yes	$680

DSLR Cameras

This is the fastest growing category of digital cameras. The SLR category of camera has been a favorite of professionals and advanced enthusiasts for decades. As the cost of high-quality Digital SLR Cameras has decreased over the last decade, these cameras have become more appealing to consumers in general. Sadly, many consumers buy these cameras and use them as if they were Point-and-Shoot cameras.

Canon & Nikon dominate this category of camera. If you want to do a lot of research or have an issue with these brands, there are other options. For most people, it makes sense to buy a Canon or Nikon DSLR as your first DSLR. It will be easier to find lenses, get bargains, and get support and advice if you have problems. Most professionals use Canon or Nikon cameras and are mostly loyal to their preferred brand.

The 40 Best-Selling DSLR Cameras on Amazon.com are all Canon and Nikon except a Sony Model at Number 35.

I'm going to start with the Canon lineup, since Canon appears to have the edge right now. **Figure 3.16** should give you some idea of how much the Sensor Size affects the size of these cameras. Unlike other categories, the Sensor size information for DSLRs is not only easy to find, it is a part of the description.

The Camera on the left in **Figure 3.16** contains the smallest Sensor used in DSLR cameras. The Camera on the right contains a Full-Frame Sensor – the largest size used in DSLR Cameras. These are the only sizes used in Nikon Cameras, but Canon has used an interim sized APS-H Sensor for some models. Also, the Nikon APS-C is slightly larger than the Canon APS-C Sensor. Take another look at **Figure 2.1**, if you need to refresh your memory about Sensor sizes.

Figure 3.16

http://en.wikipedia.org/wiki/File:Dslr_sensor_comparison.jpg
Wikipedia Commons Image

Full Frame   864 mm²
APS-H   548 mm² (Canon)
APS-C   370 mm² (Nikon)   329 mm² (Canon)

The chart below lists the Top 10 Best-Selling DSLR cameras on Amazon.com for February 16, 2013.

Rank	Mfg	Model	Lens	Sensor	MP	AF pts	Processor	Max Fps	Price
1	Canon	T3	18-55	APS-C	12.1	9	Digic 4	3	$399
2	Canon	T3i	18-55	APS-C	18	9	Digic 4	3.7	$599
3	Canon	T4i	18-55	APS-C	18	9	Digic 5	5	$649
4	Canon	T4i	18-135	APS-C	18	9	Digic 5	5	$859
5	Nikon	D5100	18-55	APS-C	16.2	11	Expeed 2	4	$597
6	Nikon	D3100	18-55	APS-C	14.2	11	Expeed 2	3	$447
7	Canon	5D Mk III	None	Full	22.3	61	Digic 5+	6	$2975
8	Canon	60D	None	APS-C	18	9	Digic 4	5.3	$700
9	Nikon	D3200	18-55	APS-C	24.2	11	Expeed 3	4	$597
10	Canon	6D	24-105	Full	20.2	11	Digic 5+	4.5	$1879

The chart provides some interesting insights into the market.

- The Full-Frame option is much more expensive than the APS-C versions.
- The 18-55 mm Lens is very popular.

- APS-C based DSLR's are relatively inexpensive and very popular.

I included AF pts (Auto-Focus Points) and Max Fps (Maximum Frames per Second) because they sometimes affect a buying decision. The 61 AF points for the Canon 5D Mark III set it apart from the other cameras in this list. Max Fps indicates the most images that can be captured in a second. This limit is a result of how fast the shutter can open and close as well as how fast the image data can be processed and recorded on the camera's memory card. AF points and maximum Fps should be a consideration if you do a lot of Freeze-Action Photography such as sporting events.

Canon Rebel T4i

I want to start our review of Canon DSLR Cameras with the Canon Rebel T4i **(Figures 3.17 thru 3.21)**. This is the latest model in the Rebel lineup and number 3 and 4 on our list above.

The T4i has received rave reviews and is generally considered a significant upgrade over the T3i. It has a faster processor and can capture more frames in a second – 5 vs 3.7. The difference in price between items 3 and 4 above is strictly the lens included with the camera. The 18-55 mm Lens is called a "Kit Lens" and basically comes free with the camera. If purchased separately it would cost about $200. The 18-135 Lens has a wider range of capability and sells for about $500 by itself. If you upgrade to this lens when you purchase the camera, you get it for about $210. Both options are a good deal.

All DSLR's have mode selectors like the Compact Cameras that we reviewed earlier. This should give you a level of comfort if you have never owned a DSLR Camera before. You can take the camera out of the box, set it on a pre-programmed mode, and shoot away, knowing that you will get some pretty good images. But the real power of these cameras comes from using them in the "Creative Modes" – Aperture Value, Time Value, and Manual. This is where you will learn the art of photography.

We will be talking about these modes and settings in a future chapter, but for now let's just assume that the ability to make manual adjustments is your purpose in buying a DSLR. With that in mind, I am not going to go through all the features – just what seems significant.

Auto-Focus / Manual Focus Selector

Image Stabilizer Selector

Figure 3.17

Canon Rebel T4i

EF-S Lens Alignment Mark

With DSLRs, Auto-Focus is switched on and off on the lens **(Figure 3.17)**. Personally, I rarely use the Auto-Focus function because it can cause problems if you aren't paying strict attention. We'll talk more about focusing later in the book.

The Lens in **Figure 3.17** has an Image Stabilizer. Not all Lenses have this feature. You want to use the stabilizer function when you use your camera hand-held, and turn it off when you use a tripod. The image stabilizer uses gyroscopes inside the lens to move lens elements in the opposite direction of lens movement. This has the effect of keeping the image blur-free at much slower shutter speeds than normally acceptable for hand-held photography.

From the little white square on the side of this lens **(Figure 3.17)**, I know that it is a Canon EF-S Lens. The white square is aligned with a white square on the lens mounting ring of the camera body **(Figure 3.18)** when it is inserted into the camera. The Lens is then rotated clockwise a few degrees until it locks in place. We will discuss Lenses in detail in the next chapter.

If this had been an EF Lens, it would have a Red Dot and align with a Red Dot on the camera's lens mounting bracket **(Figure 3.18)**.

EF Lenses fit all Canon DSLR models, but EF-S Lenses are specifically designed for the APS-C Sensor based cameras such as the Rebel product line. Because of the smaller Sensor size (compared to a Full-Frame Sensor), they can be shorter than the comparable EF Lens. The reason for this will be covered in Chapter 4, so until then let's just accept that the EF-S Lenses are smaller and less expensive than their EF counterparts.

Aligning Mark for EF Lenses

Aligning Mark for EF-S Lenses

Figure 3.18

Lens Release Button

APS-C Sensor

Canon Rebel T4i

Lens Mounting Ring

Moving to the back of the camera **(Figure 3.19)**, note the optical Viewfinder and the Diopter Adjustment that allows you to customize the Viewfinder for your eyes.

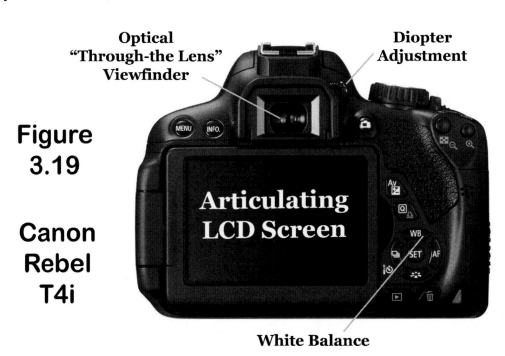

Optical "Through-the Lens" Viewfinder

Diopter Adjustment

Figure 3.19

Articulating LCD Screen

Canon Rebel T4i

White Balance

The third item noted in **Figure 3.19**, **WHITE BALANCE**, is a way to calibrate the camera's color settings. This is another topic of great interest for later in the book.

Figure 3.20

Canon
Rebel
T4i

The Articulating "Vari-Angle" LCD Touch Screen **(Figure 3.20)** makes it easier to capture images at unusual angles and the GP-E2 GPS Receiver **(Figure 3.21)** will add GPS data to your image files automatically when attached to the camera by the Hotshoe. The GP-E2 currently sells for $243 on Amazon.com.

Figure 3.21

Canon 5D Mark III

Next, let's look at a Full-Frame DSLR – the 5D Mark III **(Figures 3.22 thru 3.24)**. From the Red Dot on the lens mount **(Figure 3.22)**, we know that this camera can only use the EF Lenses.

Figure 3.22

Canon 5D Mark III

EF Lens Align-

Full-Frame Sensor

Mirror
(Locked Horizontally)

Figure 3.23

Canon 5D Mark III

Video Recording

LCD Screen

This is a professional model with fewer presets **(Figure 3.24)**. Although the camera has many upgraded features, it is the photographer who is in charge here.

Simplified Mode Selection Dial

Camera Settings

Figure 3.24

Canon 5D Mark III

Understanding Canon DSLR Model Numbers

Market	Model Example	Sensor Size	Price	Numbering Scheme	AKA
Entry Level	EOS 650D	APS-C	$648	3 or 4 Digits	Rebel / Kiss
Advanced Amateur	EOS 40D	APS-C	$1325	2 Digits	Elan 7-Series
Prosumer	EOS 5D Mark III	Full-Frame	$3149	1 Digit	
Professional / Flagship	EOS 1DX	Full-Frame	$6729	1	

Apart from Sensor Size, the greatest difference in market segments is durability of the product. The entry-level Rebel Product Line is mostly plastic wherever possible. In the Advanced Amateur group, the frame is magnesium alloy. In the top two categories, more expensive and durable materials and processes are used. Better weather sealing is also a priority in the high-end models.

I have focused on Canon Cameras because this is what I know best. Nikon has similar models and features at comparable prices. It is just a matter of doing a bit of research if you want to know more about Nikon.

My desire is to present this very complex subject as simply as possible. If you understand your options with one manufacturer it is easy to understand another. For this reason, I will be using Canon as an example more often than any other manufacturer. This is not to suggest that they are the only player – it just simplifies the discussion.

Nikon D3100

Nikon cameras will be very similar to the Canon models. The Nikon D3100 **(Figures 3.25 thru 3.27)** uses the Nikon DX Sensor which is Nikon's APS-C Sensor, and it is slightly larger than the Canon APS-C Sensor. This is a 14 MP camera that currently sells for $447 on Amazon.com. The Kit Lens is comparable to the Kit lens for the Canon Rebel T4i. Note that each manufacturer also has proprietary lenses that are designed for their cameras and certain lines of lenses work with particular lines of cameras.

Figure 3.25

Nikon D3100

Figure 3.26

Nikon D3100

Figure 3.27

Nikon D3100

Nikon Lens

Mode Selector Dial

Medium-Format Cameras

Medium-Format Cameras are usually **System Cameras**. This means that you can assemble a camera to your liking or change parts as needed **(Figure 3.28)**.

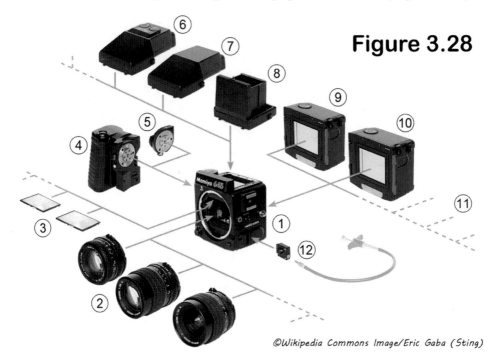

Figure 3.28

©Wikipedia Commons Image/Eric Gaba (Sting)

Hasselblad H5D-60
$42,000

Figure 3.29

This Camera CCD 2159 mm^2
2.5X Full Frame

Full Frame CMOS 864 mm^2

60 Megapixels

Hasselblad is probably the best know name in Medium-Format cameras. They were the cameras of choice for the Apollo Moon Missions. The Sensor in the Camera above **(Figure 3.29)** is 2.5 times the size of a Full-Frame Sensor in a DSLR. The Sensor is also made with the more expensive CCD technology.

Large-Format Cameras

Large-Format Film Cameras are still used for Commercial Photography, such as, ads for movies and billboards, but they are beginning to be replaced by Digital Versions **(Figure 3.30)**.

Arca Swiss f-metric 6X9 with Phase One P25

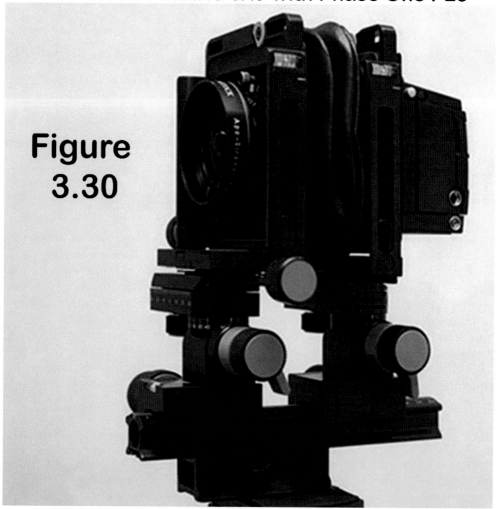

Figure 3.30

http://www.luminous-landscape.com/essays/digital-view.shtml

These cameras are much different than anything that we have discussed to this point, but they are still understandable because of our previous discussion of camera basics. So let's walk through the basics referring to **Figure 3.31.**

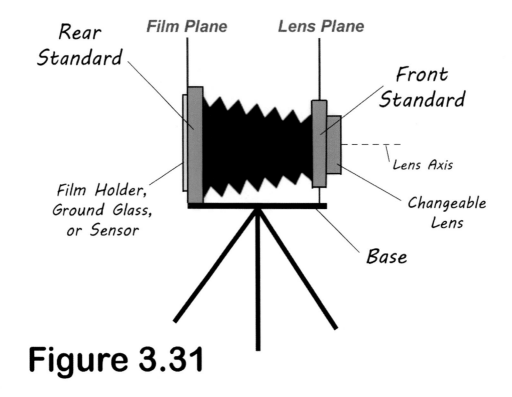

Figure 3.31

The Lens is attached to the Front Standard and the Film or Sensor is attached to the Rear Standard. The Standards can be moved and clamped anywhere along the length of a bar called the Base, which is mounted on one or more tripods. The Standards are joined by a Light-Tight collapsible bellows. The Distance between the Lens Plane and the Film Plane is the Effective Focal Length of the Lens. The Shutter for these cameras is built into the Lens and activated by a cable. The Front Standard can also be tilted and raised or lowered relative to the Rear Standard. The reasons for doing this are beyond the scope of this book, but it has to do with achieving the sharpest focus possible for the particular situation as well as eliminating perspective distortions that are common in most cameras.

Film is still very popular in these cameras. As you can see from **Figures 3.32 thru 3.33**, these cameras can be quite large. The one shown uses a 20 inch by 24-inch glass plate or sheet of film.

The largest Electronic Sensor that I am aware of is 8 inches X 8 inches – 50 times larger than a Full-Frame Sensor but still small for this category of camera. It may be some time yet before Digital Technology claims this niche.

Figure 3.32

Figure 3.33

Camera Comparisons

Based on cost alone, there is no need to include Medium-Format and Large-Format cameras in our comparison of cameras.

Figure 3.34 clearly shows that DSLR cameras have a clear advantage relative to Sensor Size and therefore image quality. The Mirrorless Compact Cameras are the only ones that can compete with the DSLR for Sensor Size, but they lack a significant choice of Lenses. Cost wise, Mirrorless is in the same ballpark as many of the APS-C based DSLRs. So, you give up the Optical Viewfinder and you get a smaller camera with more Wide-Angle Capability. For this reason, it might have been grouped with the DSLRs instead of the Compacts. Either way, with this one exception, the Compact category offers no clear advantage over the DSLR category and has some serious limitations.

For me, the DSLR is just a better investment and will make you a better photographer if you learn to use the manual controls.

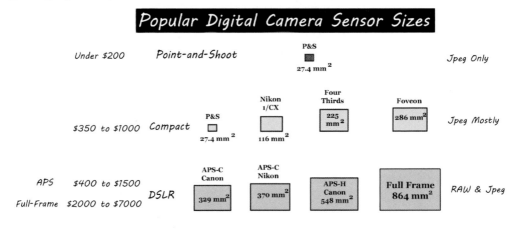

Figure 3.34

If you are in the market for your first DSLR, the Canon Rebel T4i is a great camera for the money. You may want to upgrade to a Full-Framed DSLR sometime in the future, but you will be very pleased with this camera for a long time. Just remember that it can use EF-S Lenses as well as EF Lenses. If you ever upgrade to a Canon model with a Full-Frame Sensor, the EF-S Lenses will not work on the new camera. For Nikon Cameras with APS-C Sensors, the NX Lenses perform the same function as Canon's EF-S Lenses. These Lenses are designed so that the back of the Lens projects into the body of the camera. When placed on a Full-Frame camera body, these lenses would interfere with the movement of the larger mirror. We'll take a closer look at this in Chapter Four.

Some Things to Remember

You will always be limited in the quality of the images captured with a Point-and-Shoot camera because of the very small Sensor that they use and the fact that they only save images in the Jpeg format.

Compact (Bridge) Cameras have some nice features but offer no clear advantage over DSLR cameras in price or features. This is a market segment that will appeal to a limited number of people for very specific reasons and should rarely be the primary camera.

DSLRs are the workhorse cameras of professional photographers and serious enthusiasts. This should be the camera of choice for anyone who wants to move beyond snapshots.

Medium- and Large-Format cameras should only be considered after gaining significant experience with DSLRs.

The Cropped-Frame DSLR is a great starter camera. A Kit Lens with the widest range of Focal Lengths is highly desirable. A camera like the Canon Rebel T4i with the 18 mm – 135 mm Lens is a great value for many reasons.

Canon and Nikon dominate the DSLR market for many good reasons and provide a great starting place for aspiring photographers.

Photographic Terms Introduced in this Chapter

Bridge Camera   A camera that "Bridges the Gap" between Point-and-Shoot and DSLR cameras.

System Camera   A camera that can be modified by changing parts.

Compact System Camera   A Compact Camera with changeable Lenses.

Mirrorless Camera   A Compact camera design with interchangeable Lenses that has no Mirror or Optical Viewfinder. Also known as an EVIL (Electronic Viewfinder Interchangeable Lenses) camera. This is somewhat misleading since most of these cameras have no Viewfinder at all – only an LCD Screen.

Rear Standard   A moveable frame in Large-Format Cameras that holds the photographic media – glass plate, film, or digital Sensor.

Front Standard   A moveable frame in Large-Format Cameras that holds the Lens. It can be tilted in several directions relative to the Rear Standard. It can also be moved vertically relative to the Rear Standard.

Chapter Four: Interchangeable Lenses

This might be a good time to take another look at **Figure 1.26**. There is no Lens built into a DSLR camera. DSLRs are often purchased without a lens and are designated as "Body Only" in the description. When a Lens is included in the purchase, it is called a **Kit Lens**. Sometimes there are several Kit Lens options available. Buying the camera with a Kit Lens is normally a bargain.

©iStockphoto·com/alxpin
Figure 1.26

Digital SLR Camera with 5 Lenses

The ability to change Lenses is one of the best features of DSLR cameras.

These Lenses (**Figure 1.26**) are commonly referred to as *Interchangeable Lenses*. They can be used on several different cameras and numerous Lenses can be used on a single camera. The beauty of this approach is that you can buy a Lens that best suits your photographic preferences. For example, Wedding photographers use Lenses that are quite different from those typically used by Studio Portrait Photographers. The explanation for this is beyond the scope of this book and not important at this time. For now, just remember:

Interchangeable Lenses allow photographers to optimize image quality based on the type of photography that interests them.

Unfortunately, understanding your choices in Lens selection can be quite intimidating to most novice photographers. When I was ready for my first Lens upgrade (over 30 years ago), I did not know any of the information in this Chapter and made some very bad decisions as a result. When I moved to Digital

Cameras, I had to re-educate myself because so many of these Lenses have features that were not available even ten years ago.

When I went to camera shops to ask about Lenses, I just got confused because I didn't have enough perspective to ask the right questions. I also discovered that I didn't know enough Lens terminology to understand the answers that I did get.

My intention is to make your journey a bit easier than mine. In this Chapter, I will be presenting enough information to give you a general understanding of what is available and why you might want to upgrade your current Lens. It will also give you some perspective on the Lens that came with your camera.

When you will need this information depends upon how actively you practice photography and how much experience you currently have. I just want to be sure that you know where to find the information when you need it.

In chapter one, we said:

SENSOR SIZE and LENS QUALITY are the two most important factors affecting image quality.

In **Chapter Three**, we talked about Sensor Size and how it affects image quality. If you own or buy ***any DSLR***, your Sensor will have sufficient resolution to produce some fine images.

So let's talk more about Lenses. This is no small topic. Canon currently offers 74 different Lenses for use with its DSLR cameras. The number and types will be very similar for Nikon or any other manufacturer.

Types of Lenses

Once again, to simplify our discussion, I will initially only talk about Canon Lenses. We will talk about other manufacturers later in the chapter. Before we go on, we need to talk about the three big categories of Lenses – ***Wide-Angle***, ***Normal***, and ***Telephoto***. Each of these types has a place in your camera bag, and some very specific characteristics that you should be aware of.

The next three images were captured from the exact same tripod location. I set up the shot with a particular rock formation – Coffee Pot Rock – at the center of the frame. I then changed lenses without moving the tripod or repositioning the camera in any way.

The first shot **(Figure 4. 1)** was taken at a Focal Length of 18 mm with my Wide-Angle Lens.

Figure 4.1

Wide-Angle Lens 18 mm Focal Length

The second shot **(Figure 4. 2)** was taken with a Normal Lens – 50 mm Focal Length. This type of Lens is called Normal because its 50 mm focal length simulates human vision.

Figure 4.2

Normal Lens 50 mm Focal Length

The final shot **(Figure 4. 3)** was taken with a Telephoto Zoom Lens set to a Focal Length of 250 mm.

Figure 4.3

Telephoto Lens 250 mm Focal Length

In real life, you would rarely place your object of interest in the exact center of the frame, but in this case, it helps to see the effect of changing the Focal Length.

As demonstrated in **Figure 4.1, Wide-Angle Lenses** (Focal Length of 35 mm or less) shrink objects in the background and enlarge objects close to the camera. This is why the cars and buildings in this picture stand out and the Red Rocks fade into the distance.

Figure 4.2, Normal Lenses (40 mm to 70 mm Focal Length) simulate human vision and tend to look very natural to us. In this photo, we tend to see the rock formations in the background and try to tune out the buildings in the foreground.

Figure 4.3, Telephoto Lenses (anything above a Focal Length of 80 mm) shrink distance and act like magnifying glasses. Coffee Pot Rock is about two miles from the camera, but there is no sense of distance in the image.

These natural characteristics of Lenses can be used for artistic purposes – to emphasize some detail of an image.

The photo below (**Figure 4.4**) demonstrates the use of a **Wide-Angle Lens** to *enlarge a detail in the foreground* so that it stands out against the background.

Figure 4.4

These twisted Juniper Trees in the foreground would be barely noticeable if a Normal Lens had been used.

The next photo (**Figure 4.5**) demonstrates the use of a **Telephoto Lens** to *shrink distance.*

The people in the photo are about two miles from the rock formation, but that fact is lost in the image. What does come through is the power and majesty of the huge rocks.

Figure 4.5

Before we continue our discussion of Lenses, we need to define some important terms.

A Zoom Lens is not the same as a Telephoto Lens. A **Zoom Lens** is any Lens in which the Focal Length can be varied. A **Telephoto Lens** is a Lens with a minimum Focal Length of 80 mm or more. Thus, a Zoom Lens is not necessarily a Telephoto Lens, and a Telephoto Lens is not necessarily a Zoom Lens.

A **Kit Lens** is a Lens that is included in the purchase price of a camera. For the Canon Rebel T4i this Lens is a Zoom Lens with a range of Focal Lengths from 18 mm to 55 mm. For an additional $210 you can upgrade the Kit Lens to a Zoom Lens of 18 mm to 135 mm Focal Length. The standard Kit Lens will cover the Wide-Angle and Normal ranges. The Upgrade Lens will cover all three categories – Wide-Angle, Normal, and Telephoto.

The advantage of this type of Zoom Lens is that you can start taking pictures and learn from experience what Focal Lengths you use the most often without a significant investment in Lenses.

More Definitions

EF (Electro Focus) Lenses   Canon's proprietary Lenses for its camera product line. First introduced in 1987, Canon added a motor to the lens assembly for rapid auto-focusing.

EF-S (EF with Short back focus)   This is a special product line of Canon's Lenses that work ONLY with Cropped Sensor (APS-C) Cameras like the Rebel Product Line. The **S** stands for Short Back Focus, that is, the distance from the back of the Lens to the Focal Plane or Sensor is Shorter than normal.

Figure 4.6 shows the basic principle behind EF-S Lenses.

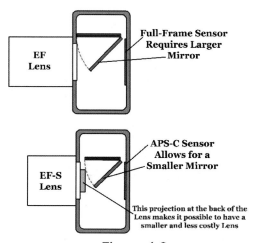

Figure 4.6

Figure 4.7 shows the actual Lenses next to each other.

Figure 4.7

EF-M   Lenses that are specifically designed for Canon's Mirrorless camera. Currently there are only two choices in this category.

Macro Lenses   Lenses that excel at close-up shots of things like bugs and flowers.

A **Prime Lens** has a fixed Focal Length. This results in smaller and less expensive Lenses. The drawback is that you would need to purchase and carry several Prime Lenses to have the same range of capability as one Zoom Lens.

Lens Extender   This is a tube that fits between the Lens and the Camera. Sometimes used with Telephoto Lenses to increase the Focal Length of the Lens. Two models are currently available for the Canon EF Lenses with magnifications of 1.4X and 2X. They cost $500 each.

Tilt-Shift Lens (TS-E)   This is a Lens that allows you to change the Perspective of an image. One popular use is to create images that look like miniature scenes. This topic is beyond the scope of this book but will be discussed in ***Book 2: The Art of Photography***. **Figure 4.8** shows a Tilt Lens and **Figure 4.9** shows a Shift Lens in use. **Figure 4.10** explains what a Shift Lens does.

Tilt

Figure
4.8

©Wikipedia Commons Image/Motorrad-67

Tilt-Shift Lenses perform the same function as the adjustments for the Front-Standard of Large-Format cameras.

Shift

Nikon

Figure
4.9

©Wikipedia Commons Image/Motorrad-67

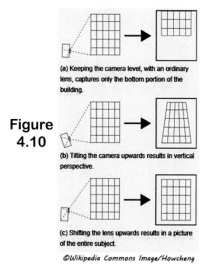

(a) Keeping the camera level, with an ordinary lens, captures only the bottom portion of the building.

Figure
4.10

(b) Tilting the camera upwards results in vertical perspective.

(c) Shifting the lens upwards results in a picture of the entire subject.

©Wikipedia Commons Image/Howcheng

Effective Focal Length

When you decide to purchase a new lens, you might run across the term, **Effective Focal Length**. This concept is a result of the fact that not all Sensors are Full-Frame. A Lens that is used on a Full-Frame camera projects the image onto the entire Sensor area. If the actual Sensor is Smaller than Full-Frame, the Sensor will not be able to capture the entire image available to it.

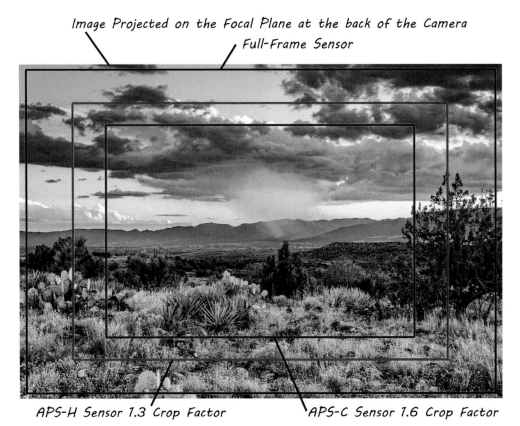

Image Projected on the Focal Plane at the back of the Camera

Full-Frame Sensor

APS-H Sensor 1.3 Crop Factor

APS-C Sensor 1.6 Crop Factor

Figure 4.11

In **Figure 4.11**, the **BLUE** box represents the size of an APS-C Sensor, and the **RED** box represents the size of an APS-H Sensor. The crop factor for each Sensor is the ratio of its diagonal to the diagonal of a Full-Frame Sensor.

If we take another look at the first three images of this chapter, superimposed upon each other, we get the image in **Figure 4.12**.

As you can see, increasing the Focal Length has a cropping effect similar to using a smaller Sensor. For this reason, it has become common to apply the Sensor cropping factor to the Focal Length to determine an equivalent Effective Focal Length. For example, a 50 mm Focal Length used with an APS-C Sensor will capture the same amount of the image as an 80 mm Focal Length when used with a Full-Frame Sensor.

50 mm X 1.6 (Cropping Factor) = 80 mm

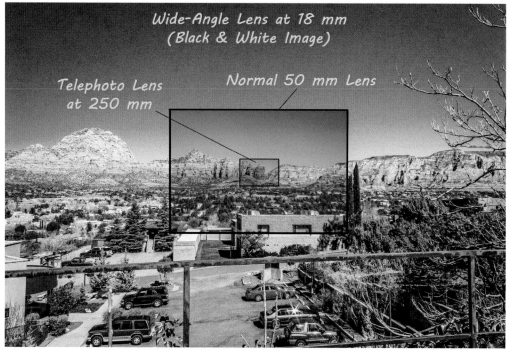

Figure 4.12

Because of this effect, wildlife photographers sometimes prefer to use a smaller APS-C Sensor camera like the Canon Rebel Series or Canon EOS 40D.

Telephoto Lenses are very expensive and get more expensive as the Focal Length increases. A 300 mm Telephoto Lens can cost around $5,000. If that Lens is used on a camera with an APS-C Sensor, it has the same effect as a 500 mm (300 mm X 1.6 = 480 mm) Lens on a Full-Frame camera. A 500 mm Lens will cost around $11,000. So, it is much less expensive to have two camera bodies – Full-Frame and Cropped-Frame – and only one Lens. Although a Full-Frame Sensor will produce a better image, the tradeoff does not justify the cost of the 500 mm Lens.

Aperture Values of Lenses

As you may recall, the Aperture is the hole formed by the Diaphragm in the camera Lens that limits how the light enters the camera. The size of the Aperture has a great deal of influence on the appearance of the image. We will be talking about this in detail in the next chapter, but for now, just remember:

For Lenses, the larger the Maximum Aperture size, the better.
Lenses can have a fixed Maximum Aperture size or a variable value. Prime Lenses (those with a *fixed* Focal Length) will always have a fixed Aperture value but Zoom Lenses can have either.

In general, Zoom Lenses with a Fixed Maximum Aperture are larger and more expensive than Zoom Lenses with variable values.

MATH ALERT!!! The following hypothetical example is not critical to our discussion but offered for those who are curious about the details of the point being made. If math is not your thing, just skip over this part.

Let's take a hypothetical example to illustrate this point: Say that the Zoom Lens covers Focal Lengths of 30 mm to 70 mm and that this particular Lens can only be set to 4 Aperture Sizes at the 50 mm Focal Length – 12 mm diameter, 6 mm diameter, 3 mm diameter, and 1.5 mm diameter.

Now imagine that these same hole sizes are the Aperture sizes at any Focal Length.

Aperture values are called f-Stops and are written as $f/4, f/11, f/22$, etc. The f stands for Focal Length and therefore $f/8$ means the Focal Length of the Lens divided by 8. Therefore, a Lens with a Focal Length of 80 mm will have an Aperture that is 10 mm in Diameter at $f/8$.

$f/8$ = Focal Length / 8 = 80 mm / 8 = 10 mm Diameter

For our hypothetical Lens, the maximum size of the Aperture is a 12 mm diameter hole.

At the shortest Focal Length of **30 mm**, this Aperture would be:

30 mm / 12 mm = $f/2.5$

At the longest Focal Length of **70 mm**, this maximum Aperture would yield:

70 mm / 12 mm = $f/5.83$

This hypothetical Lens would be designated as:

30-70 mm   f/2.5-5.8

If the lens were designed to have a maximum Aperture of $f/2.5$ across its entire Focal Length range, it would still be fine at the 30 mm focal length but would require a much larger Aperture at the 70 mm Focal Length. It would therefore need a maximum Aperture size of:

70mm / 2.5 = **28 mm diameter** and would be designated as **30-70 mm f/2.5**

Please Note: Lenses would never be designed to these f-stop values. The example above is just a hypothetical situation intended to illustrate a point.

END of MATH ALERT!!!

If I lost you in this example, don't worry about it. For now, just remember:

Zoom Lenses with a single f-stop designation are larger and more expensive than Zoom Lenses with a f-stop range designation.

Figure 4.13 illustrates the relative size of these two hypothetical Lenses.

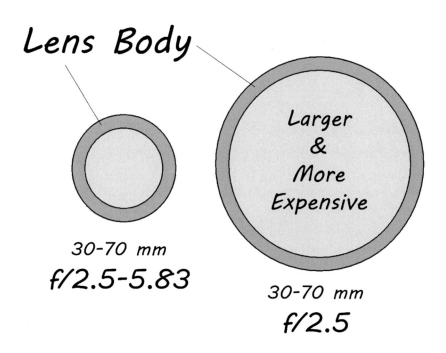

Figure 4.13

Now Let's get into the specifics of Lens selection.

Understanding Lens Designations

Canon EF-S 55-250mm f/4.0-5.6 IS II Telephoto Zoom Lens

Figure 4.14

Figure 4.14 shows a typical Canon Telephoto Zoom Lens.

Going clockwise around the Lens starting at the top right:

Minimum Focus Distance   This is the closest that you can get to an object and still be able to sharply focus this Lens. The value is normally stated in English as well as Metric units.

Current Focal Length   This indicates the focal length in millimeters selected by rotating the Zoom Adjustment Ring.

Focal Length Range   This is the range of focal lengths covered by this Lens.

Auto Focus / Manual Focus Selector   Auto Focus capability is built into the Lens but controlled by the camera when the Lens is attached.

Image Stabilizer Switch   This function is also built into the Lens and controlled by the camera processor.

Zoom Adjustment Ring   This is the large gripping area closest to the camera. You rotate it to Zoom in and out. You are actually changing the focal length of the Lens when you rotate this ring.

Focus Ring   This is a smaller gripping area toward the front of the Lens and is only rotated for manual focus. Trying to turn this ring when Auto Focus is engaged can harm both the Lens and camera.

From the Lens designation, **Canon EF-S 55-250 mm f/4.0-5.6 IS II Telephoto Zoom Lens**, we know that this is a Canon EF-S Lens – which is also obvious from looking at the projection at the back of the Lens **(Figure 4.14)** on the right side of the photo.

It is a Zoom Lens with a Focal Length Range of 55 mm to 250 mm

It has a Maximum Aperture Size of $f/4$ at the 55 mm Focal Length

It has a Maximum Aperture Size of $f/5.6$ at the 250 mm Focal Length

It has Image Stabilization (IS).

It is the Second Version of this Lens Design (II).

Before we look at our Lens options, we need to learn the language. The following terms are used for **Canon Lenses**. We will talk about other manufacturers a little later in the chapter.

Some of the terms used in the following Lenses Designations, refer to topics that are beyond our current level of understanding and will therefore not be defined at this time. By the time you need these advanced features, you will know what they mean. For many readers that day will never come, since some of these features are only used by very successful professionals who can justify the additional cost of these specialty Lenses.

USM – (Ultrasonic Motor)   Lenses with this designation Autofocus faster and quieter than regular Auto Focus Lenses. Also draw less power from the camera than AF lenses.

STM – (Stepper Motor)   Used for focusing during video recording. Better than USM at producing smooth, precise incremental movements needed for video capture, but slower at focusing during photo capture.

IS – (Image Stabilizer)   Employs a series of sensors and a high-speed microcomputer to measure the vibrations and apply corrections with a specialized lens group. Most useful when shooting hand-held at low light. Should be turned off when using a tripod. IS on/off switch is located on the body of a lens.

L-series (Luxury)   Canon's top-of-the-line lenses. Identified by a red line around the front element of the lens. Image quality is second to none. Typically heavy and expensive.

DW-R (Dust and Water Resistant)   Most L-series lenses have this construction which allows for shooting in rainy and snowy weather as well as other harsh conditions, such as sandy beaches or humid jungles.

DO (Diffractive Optics)   Compacts glass elements while keeping chromatic (color) aberration at a minimum. An example is Canon's EF 70-300 mm DO lens which is relatively small and light when compared to lenses with a similar zoom range.

Macro Lenses can focus at extremely close distances.

I/R (Inner and Rear Focusing)   Focusing is accomplished with the movement of internal lens groups, eradicating extension and rotation of the front lens element. This creates improved compactness and eases filter use. This is a benefit when using a Polarizing Filter.

TS-E (Tilt-Shift with an electromagnetic diaphragm)   Moves Focal Plane to control perspective and Depth-of-Field. Manual focus only.

FT-M (Full Time Manual focus)   Even when Autofocus is engaged.

FP (Focus Preset)   Focus distance is preset and instantly returned to.

The following three charts list all the available Canon Lenses as of February 19, 2013, according to the Canon website.

A little time spent studying these charts should increase your comfort level with understanding what is available and how to decipher the code that Canon uses to identify features and specs. It will also give you some perspective on the cost of lenses.

If you would like to print a copy of these charts for reference, please use the following link: http://www.ajphotobooks.com/mastering-digital-cameras.html to access a Pdf File containing these and other charts and illustrations from this book.

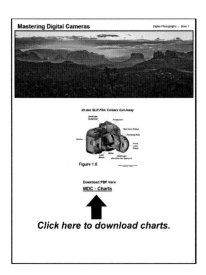

Canon Zoom Lenses

	EF	EF-S	f (mm)	f/	L	IS	II	III	USM	Other	Price
Ultra-Wide		X	10-22	3.5-4.5					X		$ 860
	X		8-15	4	X				X	Fisheye	$ 1,499
	X		16-35	2.8	X		X		X		$ 1,699
	X		17-40	4	X				X		$ 840
Standard		X	15-85	3.5-5.6		X			X		$ 800
		X	17-55	2.8		X			X		$ 1,180
		X	17-85	4-5.6		X			X		$ 600
		X	18-55	5.6		X	X				$ 200
		X	18-135	3.5-5.6		X					$ 500
		X	18-135	3.5-5.6		X				STM	$ 550
		X	18-200	3.5-5.6		X					$ 700
	X		24-70	2.8	X		X		X		$ 2,300
		X	24-70	4	X	X			X		$ 1,500
		X	24-105	4	X	X			X		$ 1,150
		X	28-135	3.5-5.6		X			X		$ 480
Telephoto	X		28-300	3.5-5.6	X	X			X		$ 2,689
		X	55-250	4-5.6		X	X				$ 300
	X		70-200	2.8	X	X	X		X		$ 2,500
	X		70-200	2.8	X	X			X		$ 2,000
	X		70-200	2.8	X				X		$ 1,450
	X		70-200	4	X	X			X		$ 1,350
	X		70-200	4	X				X		$ 710
	X		70-300	4.5-5.6		X			X	DO	$ 1,400
	X		70-300	4-5.6		X			X		$ 650
	X		70-300	4-5.6	X	X			X		$ 1,600
	X		75-300	4-5.6			III	X			$ 235
	X		75-300	4-5.6			III				$ 200
	X		100-300	4.5-5.6					X		$ 470
	X		100-400	4.5-5.6	X	X			X		$ 1,700

Canon Specialty Lenses

	EF	EF-S	f (mm)	f/	L	IS	II	III	USM	Other	Price
Tilt-Shift			17	4							$ 2,500
TS-E			24	3.5	X		II				$ 2,200
			45	2.8							$ 1,400
			90	2.8							$ 1,400
EF-M			18-55	3.5-5.6		X				STM	$ 300
			22	2						STM	$ 250

	EF	EF-S	f (mm)	f/	L	IS	II	III	USM	Other	Price
Canon Prime Lenses											
Wide-Angle	X		14	2.8	X		X		X		$ 2,359
	X		15	2.8						Fisheye	$ 720
	X		20	2.8					X		$ 540
	X		24	1.4	X		X		X		$ 1,750
	X		24	2.8		X			X		$ 850
	X		28	1.8					X		$ 510
	X		28	2.8		X			X		$ 800
	X		35	1.4	X				X		$ 1,480
	X		35	2		X			X		$ 850
	X		35	2					X		$ 320
Standard	X		40	2.8						STM	$ 200
	X		50	1.2	X				X		$ 1,620
	X		50	1.4					X		$ 400
	X		50	1.8		X					$ 126
Medium Telephoto	X		85	1.2	X				X		$ 2,200
	X		85	1.8					X		$ 420
	X		100	2					X		$ 500
Telephoto	X		135	2	X				X		$ 1,090
	X		135	2.8						Soft Focus	$ 550
	X		200	2	X	X			X		$ 6,000
	X		200	2.8	X		X		X		$ 820
	X		300	2.8	X	X			X		$ 4,880
	X		300	2.8	X		X		X		$ 7,300
	X		300	4	X	X			X		$ 1,450
Super Telephoto	X		400	2.8	X	X			X		$ 8,000
	X		400	2.8	X	X	X		X		$ 11,500
	X		400	4		X			X	DO	$ 6,470
	X		400	5.6	X				X		$ 1,340
	X		800	5.6	X	X			X		$ 14,000
	X		600	4	X	X	X		X		$ 13,000
	X		500	4	X	X	X		X		$ 10,500
Macro	X		50	2.5						Compact	$ 300
		X	60	2.8					X		$ 470
	X	MP-E	65	2.8						Photo	$ 1,050
	X		100	2.8					X		$ 600
	X		100	2.8	X	X			X		$ 1,050
	X		180	3.5	X				X		$ 1,580

Unfortunately, every manufacturer uses different codes and terms. With that in mind, I have listed Lens designations for Nikon, Sigma, Tamron, Tokina, and Zeiss.

Once again, some of the features of these Lenses are beyond the scope of this book and therefore will not be defined. My primary purpose in presenting this information is to help you decipher Lens descriptions. Some of the more advanced features will only be important after you have gained significant experience in Photography.

Nikon (Nikkor) lenses:

FX (F-mount)   For use on Full-Frame Cameras. Will fit any Nikon SLR.

DX mount   For use on cameras with APS-C sized sensors. Are typically cheaper, smaller, and lighter than FX Lenses. Fit Cropped-Frame Cameras only.

AF   Autofocus.

AF-S (Auto Focus – Silent)   Uses "Silent Wave Motor" which focuses faster and quieter than typical AF lenses. Equivalent to Canon's USM system.

AF-I (Auto Focus-Internal)   Found in older Nikkor lenses and is inferior to AF-S system.

VR (Vibration Reduction)   Similar to Canon's Image Stabilization (IS) system.

ED (Extra-low Dispersion)   Minimizes chromatic (color) aberration while effectively improving color correction and sharpness.

D (Distance/Dimension)   Conveys focus distance information to camera's computer which then calculates correct exposure. Not supported by all Nikon Cameras.

G   Must be used with Nikon DSLR body that can adjust Lens Aperture via the camera's command dial.

IF (Internal Focusing)   Similar to Canon's I/R system. Found in most modern Nikon's telephoto and zoom lenses.

Micro   For macro photography.

PC-E (Perspective Control with an electromagnetic diaphragm)
Similar to Canon's TS-E lenses.

CRC (Close-Range Correction)   Lens elements can move independently resulting in better focusing ability at close distances.

SWM (Silent Wave Motor)   Uses ultrasonic traveling waves during lens autofocus process.

N (Nano Crystal Coat)   Internal elements coated with a nano crystal solution which eliminates reflections created by most wavelength. This produces better quality images.

RF (Rear Focusing)   Creates improved compactness.

SIC (Super Integrated Coating)   Multilayer coating minimizes lens flare and ghosting (unwanted reflections).

Sigma Lenses:

DG   Similar to Canon's EF and Nikon FX mounts.

DC   For cameras with APS-C sized sensors. Like Canons EF-S and Nikon's DX mounts.

DN   For use with mirrorless interchangeable lens cameras and will not fit typical SLRs.

HSM (HyperSonic Motor)   Similar to Canon's USM and Nikon's AF-S systems.

OS (Optical Stabilization)   Similar to Canon's IS and Nikon's VR functions.

EX (Excellence)   Similar to Canon's L lenses.

APO (Apochromatic)   Similar to Nikon's ED technology.

APS (Aspherical)   Similar to Canon's DO.

RF and IF   Comparable to Canons I/R and Nikons IF technologies.

HF (Helical Focusing)   Keeps front element of a lens from rotating. Especially useful when using filters.

Tamron lenses:

Di (Digitally Integrated)   Similar to Sigma DG

Di II   Similar to Sigma DC

Di III   Similar to Sigma DN

PZD (Piezo Drive)   Similar to Sigma HSM

USD (Ultrasonic Silent Drive)   Like Canon's USM and Nikon's AF-S technologies.

VC (Vibration Compensation)   Comparable to Canon's IS and Nikon's VR.

SP (Super Performance)   Similar to Canon's L lenses.

LD   stands for Low Dispersion elements.

IF   stands for Internal Focusing.

Tokina Lenses:

FX   Similar to Canon's EF and Nikon's FX mounts.
DX.   Similar to Canon's EF-S and Nikon's DX mounts.

AT-X Pro   A line of lenses created with extra attention to quality for professionals.

AT-X   Lenses for typical consumers. Usually lighter and cheaper.

IF   Internal Focusing system.

FE (Floating Element)   Corrects astigmatism from minimum-focus distance to infinity.

AS (Aspherical Optics)   Corrects for aspherical aberration as well as light quality and distortion.

F&R (Advanced Aspherical Optics)   Provides even illumination in the corners and correction of spherical aberration throughout the entire image.

SD (Super-low Dispersion)   Eliminates chromatic aberration.

HLD (High-Refraction and Low-Dispersion)   Helps to eliminate chromatic aberration in wide-angle lenses.

MC (Multi-Coating)   Helps to eliminate lens elements' surface reflections, improving image quality.

FC (Focus Clutch)   Allows for switching the lens between auto focus and manual focus modes.

Zeiss Lenses:

ZE   Compatible with Canon's EF mounts.

ZF.2   Compatible with Nikon's F mounts.

ZA   Compatible with Sony's Alpha mounts.

T*   Indicates anti-reflective coating which improves image quality in numerous lighting conditions.

Some Things to Remember

The ability to change Lenses is one of the best features of DSLR cameras. Interchangeable Lenses allow photographers to optimize image quality based on the type of photography that interests them.

SENSOR SIZE and **LENS QUALITY** are the two most important factors affecting image quality.

The three big categories of Lenses – *Wide-Angle*, *Normal*, and *Telephoto* – all have a place in your camera bag.

Wide-Angle Lenses (Focal Length of 35 mm or less) shrink objects in the background and enlarge objects close to the camera.

Normal Lenses (40 mm to 70 mm Focal Length) simulate human vision. The term *Standard* is also sometimes used for this type of lens.

Telephoto Lenses (anything above a Focal Length of 80 mm) shrink distance and act like magnifying glasses.

The inherent optical characteristics of Lenses can be used for artistic purposes – to emphasize some detail of an image.

Effective Focal Length is a term applied to Lenses that are used on a camera with a Cropped-Frame Sensor. The formula is Focal Length X Crop Factor = Effective Focal Length.

For Lenses, the larger the Maximum Aperture size (i.e., $f/1.2$), the better.

Lenses can have a fixed Maximum Aperture size or a variable value. Prime Lenses will always have a fixed value, but Zoom Lenses can have either.

Zoom Lenses with a single f-stop designation are larger and more expensive that normal Zoom Lenses.

Photographic Terms Introduced in this Chapter

Kit Lens   The Interchangeable Lens that is offered at the time of purchase with the camera body for DSLR cameras. There is often a choice of Kit Lenses at different price points. Purchasing a Lens with the camera body often represents a savings of several hundred dollars.

Macro Lens   A Lens that is specifically designed for close-up photography of small subjects, such as flowers and bugs.

Prime Lens   A Lens that has a fixed Focal Length. It has no Zoom capability.

Lens Extender Tube   A cylindrical tube that is mounted between a Lens and the Camera Body. Its purpose is to change the focal length of the Lens by a specified factor, for example, 1.4X.

Tilt-Shift Lens   A Lens that can be Tilted or Shifted relative to the Sensor so that it changes normal perspective. Used to eliminate normal perspective distortions that are common in regular lenses.

Cropping Factor,   The ratio of the Diagonal Measurement of a given Sensor to the Diagonal Measurement of a Full-Frame Sensor.

Effective Focal Length   Focal Length X Cropping Factor of Sensor being used.

There are many terms defined in this chapter that do not appear in this list of definitions, because they apply to specific manufacturers.

Only definitions that apply to digital photography in general were included in this list.

Chapter Five: Understanding the Exposure Triangle

So far, we have established that Sensor Size and Lens Quality are the two most important contributors to Image Quality. So now, it is time to take a closer look at light. After all, photography is basically recording how light is reflected from an object.

In *Book 2: The Art of Photography*, we will talk about the artistic use of light, but for now we are more interested in the **QUANTITY OF LIGHT** that strikes the Sensor. This is commonly referred to as **EXPOSURE** and is controlled by several factors. The three most important factors are Aperture, Shutter Speed, and ISO. These three adjustments are known as the **EXPOSURE TRIANGLE (Figure 5.1)** since they work together to properly expose an image.

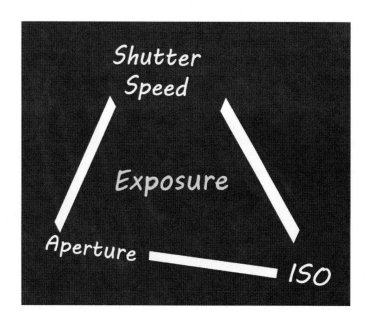

Figure 5.1

The Exposure Triangle

What is ISO?

ISO (International Standardization Organization) is another carryover term from Film Photography. It refers to the light sensitivity of Film or any other Photographic material, such as a Sensor. When the standard was established, the slowest film in common usage was Labeled ISO 100. The slowest film was the one that required the longest time to achieve proper exposure. A film that was twice as sensitive to light was Labeled ISO 200 and required half as much light to achieve the same Exposure as ISO 100. A film that was twice as sensitive to light as ISO 200 was labeled ISO 400, and so on. Thus, a photographer could choose a film with light sensitivity that was appropriate to the task at hand.

The only downside to using higher ISO film was that it had a grainy appearance when images were enlarged. The higher the ISO value, the more likely that the graininess would be noticeable. To change ISO with a film camera, you had to remove the current roll of film and replace it with a new roll of the proper ISO value. This resulted in a lot of wasted film and time. It also required a photographer to carry a lot of extra film.

With DSLR cameras, changing ISO is as simple as making a menu selection. Nothing happens to the Sensor physically, but the Sensor signal is amplified electronically as the ISO increases. Just as with Film, ISO 200 is twice as sensitive to light as ISO 100 and ISO 3200 is twice as sensitive as ISO 1600.

Take note of the fact that the ratings are based on a factor of two. ISO 800 is 2 times as sensitive as ISO 400, but half as sensitive as ISO 1600.

All things related to EXPOSURE use this same two-to-one relationship.

Aperture

The Aperture setting is probably the most important adjustment on your camera. As we learned in Chapter 1, Aperture merely means hole. It is the hole through which the light travels to create an image on the Sensor or Film. It limits the amount of light that passes through the Lens and onto the Sensor. It also has a lot to do with the Mood of the image and how much of the image is in sharp focus.

Aperture sizes are expressed in ***f-stops***. This scale can be confusing at first but is not very complicated. Basically, the size of the Aperture Opening is expressed as a fraction. It is the ***Focal Length*** (*f*) of the Lens divided by the ***Diameter*** of the Aperture. For example, if the Focal Length is 50 mm and the Diameter of the Aperture is 12.5 mm:

Focal Length / Aperture Diameter = 50 mm / 12.5 mm = 4 or f/4

Since we are using a fractional scale, *f*/8 is larger than *f*/22, just as 1/100 is larger than 1/1000.

The basic Aperture Scale is:

f/1.4   *f*/2   *f*/2.8   *f*/4   *f*/5.6   *f*/8   *f*/11   *f*/16   *f*/22

These values represent the relative AREA of the Aperture Opening and are called Full-Stops. Each stop on the scale doubles the AREA of the Aperture value to its left. Each value differs from its adjacent values by a factor of 2. In other words, the ***Area*** of the opening for ***f/5.6*** is ***twice*** that of ***f/8*** and half of ***f/4***.

Remember:

All things related to EXPOSURE use this same two-to-one relationship.

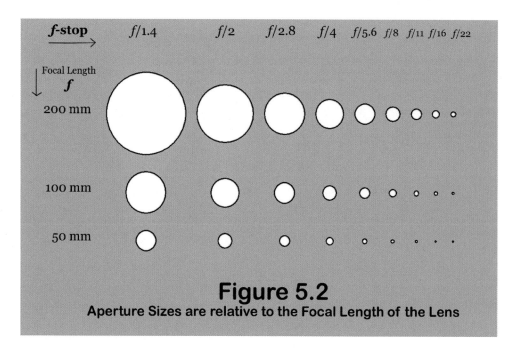

Figure 5.2
Aperture Sizes are relative to the Focal Length of the Lens

Figure 5.2 demonstrates the effect of Focal Length on Aperture Size. It also shows the dramatic difference in size between $f/1.4$ and $f/22$. $f/1.4$ is 256 times as large as $f/22$ for a given Focal Length.

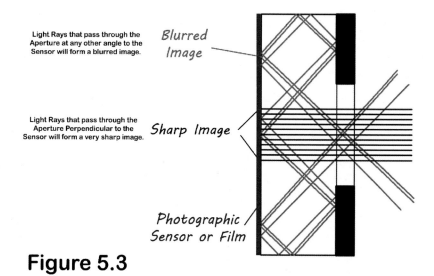

Figure 5.3

When light passes through an Aperture (**Figure 5.3**), the rays that are perpendicular to the Sensor or Film will form a very sharp image on the Sensor or film. The rays that enter the camera at any other angle will bounce around the

pg. 105

inside and interfere with other light rays. The result is a blurred image except for the area where the rays are perpendicular to the Sensor.

If the Aperture is very small – $f/22$ – most of the rays will act like the Black horizontal lines in **Figure 5.3**, thus creating a very sharp image. This is a typical Aperture setting for Landscape Photography. It will produce a sharply focused image from foreground to background.

If the Aperture is very large – $f/1.4$ – most of the rays will act like the Red diagonal lines in **Figure 5.3**. In this case, only a portion of the image will be in sharp focus. This is a great Aperture setting for Portraits. The subject will be sharply focused while the background will just be a blur. This increases attention on the subject.

This effect is called **DEPTH-OF-FIELD (DOF)**. The large Aperture produces a Shallow Depth-of-Field, and the small Aperture produces a large Depth-of-Field.

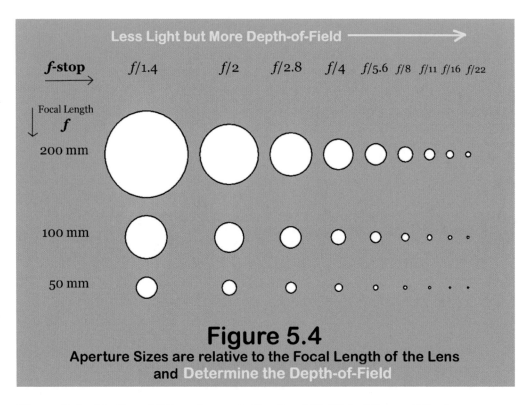

Figure 5.4
Aperture Sizes are relative to the Focal Length of the Lens and Determine the Depth-of-Field

Figure 5.4 adds the additional aspect, Depth-of-Field, to **Figure 5.2**. As you can see Depth-of-Field increases as the Aperture gets smaller. In other words, a larger percentage of the image will be in sharp focus as the Aperture gets smaller.

Figure 5.5 and **Figure 5.6** are great examples of proper Aperture selection.

Figure
5.5

Large Aperture

Nicely Blurred
Background

© Darlene Jansen 2012

Figure 5.5 has a nice soft glow to it. Our young model is in focus while the background is nicely blurred. Notice how you are immediately drawn to her eyes. This is good composition as well as good technique. The closest point to the camera that is in focus (her shoulder) is only inches away from the farthest point that is in focus (her hair). This is why we say, the image has a shallow Depth-of-Field. A large Aperture was used to create this effect.

Figure
5.6

Small Aperture

Sharp Focus
Foreground to
Background

© Darlene Jansen 2012

The old barn in **Figure 5.6** is the center of attention but notice that the grass and gravel in the foreground are also in focus. There is significant distance captured in this image and everything is in focus. We say that this image has a large Depth-of-Field.

Shutter Speed

Shutter Speed – the length of time that the Shutter is *open* – is the third and final variable in the Exposure Triangle. Shutter Speeds are expressed in fractions of a second, except for long exposures when they can be expressed in seconds or minutes.

Let's start by limiting our discussion to Shutter Speeds of less than a second.

Your settings will include values that vary by a factor of two. For example:

1/15 1/30 1/60 1/125 1/250 1/500 1/1000 1/2000 1/4000

Remember:

All things related to EXPOSURE use this same two-to-one relationship.

The fastest Shutter Speeds are used to stop motion – like a dancer in mid-air or a receiver catching a football. Slower Shutter Speeds allow more light to strike the Sensor. This in turn makes it possible to close down the Aperture and create a sharper image.

It is this trade-off between Aperture and Shutter Speed that we are most often trying to balance.

Exposures of more than a second are often used at night to capture city lights or the night sky. They are also used to give flowing water a silky look.

Figure 5.7

Small Aperture
f/32

3.2 Second
Shutter Speed

Exposure Stops

When we talked about Aperture, we also talked about *f*-stops. As you may recall, *f*/5.6 is twice the area of *f*/8 and the difference is 1 Stop. Since ISO and Shutter Speed also use two-to-one increments, they can be related to Aperture by Stops. This makes it possible to mix and match settings from all three factors to achieve the desired exposure, mood, or effect.

Most often you will be concerned with balancing Aperture and Shutter Speed, so let's start there. **Figure 5.8** illustrates how these two factors can be varied to create the same exposure (Quantity of Light).

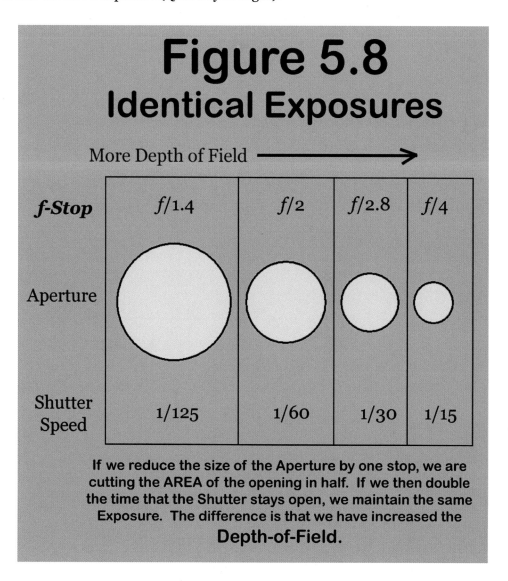

If we reduce the size of the Aperture by one stop, we are cutting the AREA of the opening in half. If we then double the time that the Shutter stays open, we maintain the same Exposure. The difference is that we have increased the

Depth-of-Field.

If you are unable to achieve the desired exposure, you can then consider ISO as another adjustment. ISO has no effect upon the light entering the camera or reaching the Sensor; it merely changes the *sensitivity* of the Sensor. You should set your ISO to ISO 100 and leave it there unless you are faced with a challenge that requires a faster Shutter Speed than you can get with ISO 100.

Common uses for high ISO are shooting indoors with dim lighting (a child blowing out candles on a birthday cake), the night sky, and outdoor objects in the shadows.

There are two more ways that you can affect the exposure – **Exposure Compensation** and **Neutral Density Filters**. A detailed discussion of these adjustments is beyond the scope of this book, but you should know that they exist. Both controls use a scale that is related to Aperture stops. This makes it easy to incorporate them into your exposure adjustments.

Remember:

All things related to EXPOSURE use this same two-to-one relationship.

Figure 5.9

Adjustment	Initial Value	One Stop	Two Stops	Three Stops	Four Stops
Aperture	f/5.6	f/4	f/2.8	f/2	f/1.4
Shutter Speed	1/500	1/250	1/125	1/60	1/30
ISO	100	200	400	800	1600
Exposure Compensation	-2	-1	0	+1	+2
Neutral Density Filters	ND32	ND16	ND8	ND4	ND2

Increase Exposure - More Light - Brighter Image $\longrightarrow$

$\longleftarrow$ Decrease Exposure - Less Light - Darker Image

Conclusion

Understanding and adjusting exposure is a significant part of becoming a competent photographer and artist. I have attempted to cover the basics here without overwhelming you. This should be enough to get you started taking great pictures. When you are ready for more information on this topic, I have written a book that goes into a lot more detail. It is:

Mastering Aperture, Shutter Speed, ISO and Exposure

Some Things to Remember

All things related to **EXPOSURE** use this same two-to-one relationship.

DEPTH-OF-FIELD (DOF) is related to Aperture Size. A large Aperture produces a Shallow Depth-of-Field, and a small Aperture produces a large Depth-of-Field.

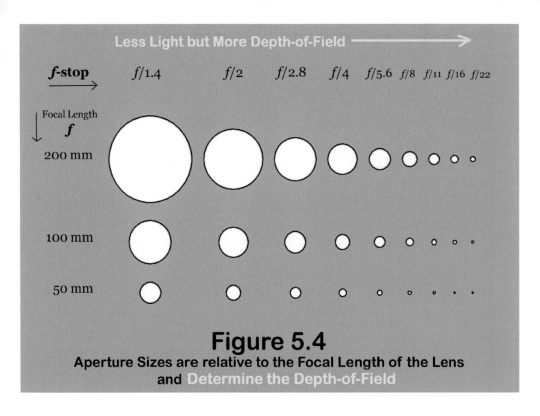

Figure 5.4

Aperture Sizes are relative to the Focal Length of the Lens and Determine the Depth-of-Field

It is this trade-off between **Aperture** and **Shutter Speed** that we are most often trying to balance.

Figure 5.9

Adjustment	Initial Value	One Stop	Two Stops	Three Stops	Four Stops
Aperture	f/5.6	f/4	f/2.8	f/2	f/1.4
Shutter Speed	1/500	1/250	1/125	1/60	1/30
ISO	100	200	400	800	1600
Exposure Compensation	-2	-1	0	+1	+2
Neutral Density Filters	ND32	ND16	ND8	ND4	ND2

Increase Exposure - More Light - Brighter Image ⟶

⟵ Decrease Exposure - Less Light - Darker Image

Photographic Terms Introduced in this Chapter

Exposure Triangle   Aperture, Shutter Speed, and ISO settings. These factors determine the amount of light available to the Sensor to produce a properly exposed image.

Exposure Compensation   An adjustment on Digital cameras used to compensate for shortcomings of the camera's built-in exposure meter.

Neutral Density Filters   A type of filter that screws onto the front of camera lenses. These filters are gray glass and have no effect on color but reduce the amount of light entering the lens. With respect to colored light or images, shades of gray will only lighten or darken. Gray does not change the color in any way. They are rated in stops so that they can easily be used to change exposure. ND Filters are often used in bright sunlight to allow for longer Shutter Speeds or larger Aperture Settings.

Chapter Six: White Balance and Other Digital Camera Controls

There are several settings that your camera will make automatically. In most cases, these settings will work beautifully. When they don't, you should know how to take control.

White Balance

WHITE BALANCE is a way to calibrate color in digital images. It can be done after the fact, in photo editing software like Photoshop and Lightroom, but is better done at the time of capturing the image. The intent is to show white as white regardless of the light source. Our eyes do this without us ever noticing, but camera Sensors are more literal in their interpretation and often add a color cast to the image based on the light source.

We all have encountered the concept of "red hot" and "white hot." The difference between the two is a matter of temperature. The object is hotter when it is white. At one point in Photographic History, a group of experts gathered to jointly assign a temperature value to various types of light. For this reason, you will often hear the term **COLOR TEMPERATURE** with respect to artificial lighting. For example, you might buy a photographic bulb rated at 5300° Kelvin.

DSLRs and some other Digital Cameras will allow you to select a White Balance for your light source. For example, you might choose Daylight or Tungsten from your White Balance Menu. This will get you in the ballpark, but as you can see in **Figure 6.1**, there is a fairly large range for each of these sources. Also note that the lower temperatures are warm, and the higher temperatures are cool.

Figure 6.1

Temperature Range			Source		Color Cast	
° Kelvin						
1000	2000		Candle Light		Warm	Red
2500	3500		Tungsten Bulb			
3000	4000		Sunrise / Sunset			
4000	5000		Fluorescent Bulb			
5000	5500		Electronic Flash			
5000	6500		Daylight			
6500	8000		Overcast			
9000	10000		Shade or Heavy Overcast		Cool	Blue

Most people, myself included, would expect Daylight to have the highest value on this scale since it is the brightest light. This is not true because the scale is related to the COLOR of the Light and not its intensity. Unfortunately, I cannot explain why overcast skies and shade are higher on the scale than Sunlight. I do know from experience that this is true. When you start using software to process your images, this will make more sense.

Your camera's Sensor assumes that the average value of any image is 18% gray. If you are trying to take a photo of fall colors and you have framed your image such that red and orange dominate, the camera will give it a bluish color cast in an attempt to achieve an 18% gray average.

In most cases your Auto-White Balance will work fine, but if you have any doubt, it is always a good idea to include a **NEUTRAL (18%) GRAY CARD** in at least one photo taken under the same lighting conditions. In photo editing software, you can select that card as your neutral gray reference, and it will give an exact temperature and tint for that photo. You can then use that same value for all other photos taken under the same conditions.

During the photo shoot itself, if you take a close up of the Neutral Gray Card that totally fills the camera's viewfinder; you can use that image to create a **CUSTOM WHITE BALANCE** reference for that shoot. Instead of selecting Daylight or any other White Balance (WB) reference, you would choose "custom." That reference would then be used until you change it.

Auto-Focus

If you use Auto-Focus on a DSLR, the toggle switch will be on the Lens (**Figure 6.2**). Auto-Focus is particularly useful when you are trying to photograph a moving subject, like a dancer or basketball player. It is not likely, in these situations, that the subject will stay in focus for long enough to even consider manual focus.

Figure 6.2

Auto-Focus / Manual Focus Selector

Image Stabilizer Switch

Figure 6.3 shows a typical 9-point pattern of Auto-Focus Points. Your camera might have anywhere from 3 to 61 points; however, 9 points is fairly common. You will be able to choose the center point, any other point, or all the points. If you chose all the points, the camera will select several of the points that relate to the closest objects in the picture. When you press the Shutter Release Button halfway down, points that are in focus will flash in your viewfinder. If you are satisfied with these points, just press the button the rest of the way to capture the image. If you select only one point, make sure that it flashes when it is over the main subject of your image. If you press the Shutter Release Button halfway, it will lock in this focus setting and allow you to reframe your image before pressing the button all the way. This is particularly helpful when you are using just the center point to focus since you will rarely want your main subject to be dead center in the frame.

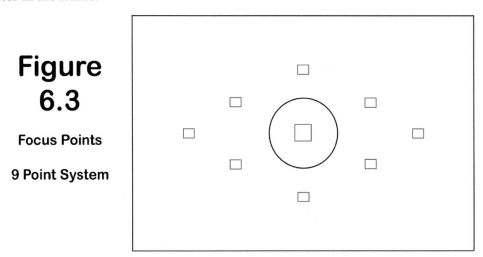

Figure 6.3

Focus Points

9 Point System

If you are photographing still objects – Landscapes or Architecture, for example – you might want to use Auto-Focus to get you in the ballpark and then fine tune the focus manually.

If you are taking a series of photos with the intention of "stitching" them together, Manual Focus will prevent the camera from focusing on some nearby object in the frame that you might not have even noticed. This is a lesson that I learned the hard way.

Auto-Exposure

Your DSLR will have a built-in exposure meter that will help you with exposure in all modes except **MANUAL.** In Manual Mode you set everything – ISO, Aperture, and Shutter Speed – to achieve proper exposure.

For my camera – a Canon – I have four choices in how the meter evaluates the required exposure. The first of those choices is called **EVALUATIVE** and is generally your best bet. With this mode (**Figure 6.4**), the image is divided into 35 zones. The camera's computer compares the tonal values of each zone to thousands of images in its database and makes an educated guess about the nature of the image. It also places extra emphasis on the zones that contain active Focus Points. For example, if the upper half of the image is bright and blue, there is a good chance that the image is a Landscape. Once the camera has made some decisions about the nature of the image, it averages the tonal values and sets the exposure. Its accuracy is quite amazing in most cases.

There are times when this method will not give you the result that you desire. One such case is when there is a very bright background. An example would be a portrait taken with the rising or setting sun directly behind the person. In the Evaluative mode, the camera averages tonal values and would choose an exposure that optimizes the background, leaving the subject in the shadows.

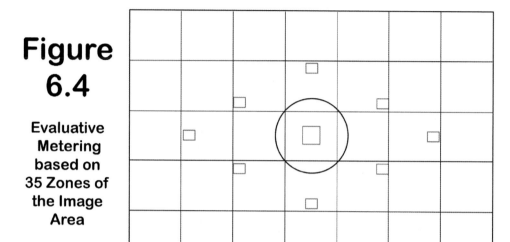

Figure 6.4

Evaluative Metering based on 35 Zones of the Image Area

PARTIAL METERING (Figure 6.5) and **SPOT METERING (Figure 6.6)** both help with bright backgrounds. Spot Metering will usually be your better choice. With a little practice, you will know which option to choose. The larger (blue) circle in **Figure 6.5** indicates the area used for Partial metering and is not something that is visible in your viewfinder. The blue circle in **Figure 6.6** indicates the area used in Spot Metering and is visible in the Viewfinder.

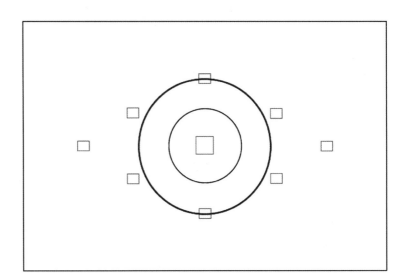

Figure 6.5

Partial Metering based on 9% of the Image Area

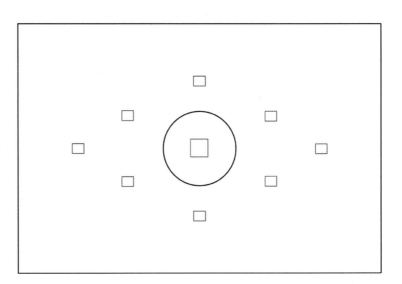

Figure 6.6

Spot Metering based on 3.5% of the Image Area

Figure 6.7 illustrates the fourth metering method available. It is called **CENTER-WEIGHTED** and uses the whole frame but places more emphasis on the center of the frame. The farther from the center, the less important the image data. This is one to consider after trying the other three. I can only suggest that you learn to use this option by trial and error.

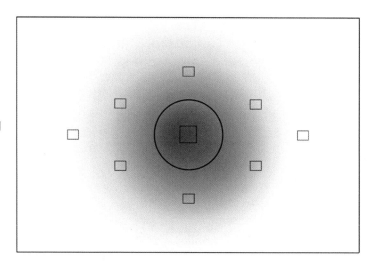

Figure 6.7

Center-Weighted Metering based on Full Frame with Emphasis on the Center

Remote Shutter Release

A remote Shutter Release is a wonderful thing to carry in your camera bag. I use a tripod about 99% of the time and am a firm believer in taking this extra measure to get the sharpest images that I can.

If you are using a tripod, you should never actually touch the camera to capture an image. You should always use some type of remote. **Figure 6.8** shows three options:

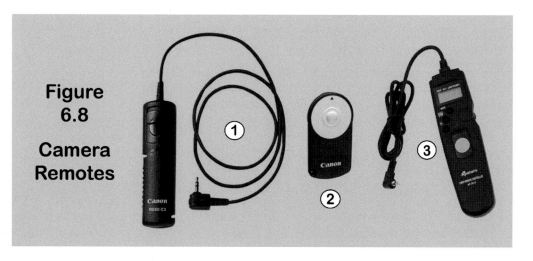

Figure 6.8

Camera Remotes

Items (**1**) and (**3**) in **Figure 6.8** plug into the side of the camera. Item (**2**) is wireless and operates on an inexpensive watch battery. I have yet to replace the battery and I have taken thousands of photos using mine.

I own all three of these items.

Item (**1**) is the basic remote and functions the same as the Shutter Release Button on your camera. This particular model currently sells for $23.37 on Amazon.com (http://tinyurl.com/a9wkwmu). It does not use a battery and therefore is a great backup device in the event that my wireless remote battery dies.

Item (**2**) is my workhorse. I rarely touch the shutter button, except for hand-held shots which are also rare. It is a little less expensive than the basic (**1**) remote – $21.70 at this time (http://tinyurl.com/b6heuzr).

Item (**3**) is a Timer Remote and is used to take photos at a regular interval. You set the exposure time and the interval between exposures as well as the total run time. Once you press the start button, you just sit back and let the camera do the work. I have used this remote to capture sunsets and sunrises. Lighting changes rapidly in these situations and by capturing a series of shots, you can pick the shot with the best lighting after the fact. I have also used this device for lightning and moonrises. Many people use these to create time-lapse sequences. It is a great investment – currently $34.95 (http://tinyurl.com/b5eglg8).

Color Space

A **COLOR SPACE (Figure 6.9)** is a range of possible colors. The area labeled "2200 Matt Paper" is not relevant to our discussion and will be ignored. The triangle labeled sRGB in **Figure 6.9** is the Color Space for the Internet and Jpeg images. This means that there is a limit to how many color variations can be captured or displayed. Low-end cameras, like Point-and-Shoot models, are only capable of capturing this range of color.

A more extensive range of colors is the Adobe RGB Color Space (also known as RGB 98 because it was developed in 1998). Adobe RGB is used by most professionals and serious enthusiasts. It produces more image detail than sRGB.

The largest Color Space is ProPhoto RGB, and it is used by some professionals. This Color Space is so large that there are no monitors or printers capable of displaying this range at this time. The professionals who use it are betting on the possibility that new technology will allow them to use this range in the future. For now, they are only capturing this range with their cameras and preserving it for future use. They can still view and print their images as if they had used a smaller Color Space.

Figure 6.9

Color Space Options

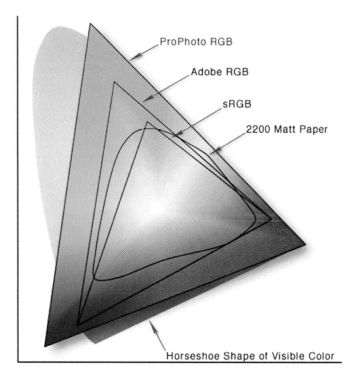

ProPhoto RGB

Adobe RGB

sRGB

2200 Matt Paper

Horseshoe Shape of Visible Color

©En·Wikipedia Commons Image/Cpesacreta

My recommendation is to set your camera to Adobe RGB if you have that option.

Highlight Tone Priority

There are situations where a portion of the frame is much brighter than the rest of the image. An example would be photographing a well-lit room with a large window in the picture. If the view through the window is of interest, it would be nice to get both the room detail and the window view properly exposed. **HIGHLIGHT TONE PRIORITY** will help you to accomplish that goal.

This will be a special menu setting, so you may have to consult your manual to find it.

Auto Lighting Optimizer

If you have a situation where everything in your picture is muted and there is very little contrast, you can punch it up by using the **AUTO LIGHTING OPTIMIZER** setting.

This will also be a special menu selection that might require the use of your owner's manual.

Photographic Terms Introduced in this Chapter

White Balance   A way of calibrating a Digital Camera so that whites in an image look white. It also calibrates all other colors.

Color Temperature   A temperature scale related to the warmth or coldness of a lighting source. Common lighting sources have specific value ranges on this scale.

Neutral Gray Card   An 18% gray card that is sometimes used to set White Balance. It is difficult to identify pure black or white in an image, but easy to find a shade of gray.

Custom White Balance   A camera setting based on a Neutral Gray Card or its equivalent, used to establish the proper White balance or Color Temperature for a given lighting condition.

Evaluative Metering AE (Auto-Exposure)   An exposure meter setting that divides the frame into several zones. Those zones are then used to calculate an average tonal value that can be related to an exposure setting.

Partial Metering AE   Exposure based on 9% of the frame and located in the center of the frame.

Spot Metering AE   An exposure setting based on a small circle at the center of the frame – approximately 3.5% of the total area of the frame. Often used to properly expose a person's face when there is a bright background.

Center-Weighted Metering AE   An exposure metering method that places more attention on the center of the frame.

Color Space   A range of possible colors captured by digital cameras and displayed by monitors. Also, a range of colors that can be printed.

Highlight Tone Priority   Balances exposure when there is a relatively large bright area in the image.

Auto Lighting Optimizer   Adds contrast and definition to dark and flat images.

Chapter Seven: Parting Thoughts and Recommendations

By now, you should have a good idea of how digital cameras work and how you might want to invest your time and money with respect to photography. You may have developed some strong preferences or opinions in the process of reading this book, but I thought that I might offer some experienced-based thoughts of my own.

If you have recently decided that Point-and-Shoot photography just isn't good enough anymore, you should definitely go shopping for a DSLR camera. If money is no object, you may want to go directly to a Professional model and spend $6,000 to $10,000 for a camera, lens, and tripod. If you are like most of us, the initial investment in a DSLR camera is a little scary. We all want to make a good decision, but we can only rely on the opinions of others until we have actual experience. We might not have the money to buy a different camera if we make a mistake. With that in mind, I would never urge anyone to buy a specific camera or lens.

What I can do, however, is share what I would do if I were just starting out. As previously mentioned, Lenses will ultimately be a bigger expense than a camera. So why not get a relatively inexpensive camera and see where it takes you. The Rebel T4i and the Nikon D5100 are very good entry level cameras. They have comparable Kit Lenses but vary slightly on price, Megapixels, and Sensor size.

Camera	Megapixels	Sensor Size	Price
Canon T4i	18.0	329 mm²	$649
Nikon D5100	16.2	370 mm²	$597

The image quality should be in the same ballpark based on the fact that Canon offers more Megapixels and Nikon has a slightly larger Sensor.

For $859 you can get the Canon Rebel T4i with an 18-135 mm Lens. I was not able to find a comparable deal on the Nikon D5100. So, I would lean toward the $859 Rebel T4i. There are several reasons for this opinion:

- If you look at reviews on Amazon.com there is no clear choice indicated, but if you read reviews by camera magazines, the T4i comes highly recommended.
- Canon currently dominates the Digital SLR market.
- The 18-135 mm Lens will allow you to experiment with a wide range of situations and discover for yourself what type of Lenses you want.
- You will only need to carry one lens with you until you gain more experience. It covers Wide-Angle, Normal, and Telephoto situations.

- You will not have to change lenses in the field and therefore are much less likely to miss a shot or get dirt on your Sensor.
- Since it is an EF-S Lens, its maximum Equivalent Focal Length is 216 mm (135 mm X 1.6 crop factor) – a very respectable Telephoto Lens.
- The image quality will be good enough to win photo contests and compete with professionals.
- The camera is much smaller and lighter than a Professional grade camera.
- You will be able to invest in some Photo Editing Software and still stay under $1000 total investment.
- Your images will gain more from Photo Editing than from a larger Sensor.
- This camera should satisfy your needs for a long time. You will need to take lots of photos before you develop an eye that is critical enough to tell the difference between an APS-C Sensor and a Full-Frame Sensor.

The only downside is that your camera will not be as durable as more expensive DSLRs, and you may not have as many features.

In ***Book 2: The Art of Photography***, we will be talking about photographic situations and choosing the right Lens and Exposure settings. This will add to your knowledge and may result in additional investments in Lenses or a camera body, but you can gain a great deal of experience and expertise with an "Entry Level" camera like the Rebel T4i or Nikon D5100.

Coming Full Circle

In the introduction, I suggested that you visit Darlene Jansen's website (***http://www.darlenejansen.smugmug.com/***) and pick your favorite photos. If you still have that list, this might be a good time to take another look at those photos. This time, study them in detail. Pay attention to the lighting and ask yourself how you would set the Aperture and Shutter Speed for that particular situation. Save your list, so that you can take another look after Books 2 and 3. You will be surprised at how much more aware you will have become of every detail.

About this Series of Books

When I started this book, I had planned to write a single book that would cover everything that any serious photographer might need to know. As I got into putting my thoughts on paper, I realized that the book would be much longer than I had imagined. I decided to split it into a series rather than eliminate material or illustrations. If you are reading this before the series is complete, I apologize for the delay. I will publish Books 2 and 3 as quickly as I can without compromising quality of content.

If you would like to know when the other books are available, send an email to **ajudex@hotmail.com** with **New Books** in the subject line. I will send you an email as soon as I finish each book. Also, if you just want to share your opinions or suggest improvements, I greatly value feedback. I will not use your email address for any other reason.

To learn about my other books, please visit my Author Page on Amazon.com **amazon.com/author/al.judge**

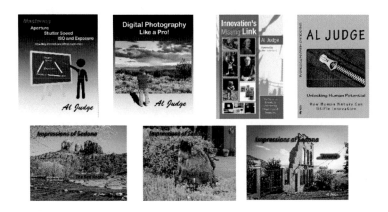

Why Reviews Help Everybody

If you found this book of value, please help others to find it by writing a review. Reviews don't have to be long – Amazon only requires 20 words.

There are over a Million eBooks and over 20 million Printed Books on Amazon.com. For an author like me, it is very difficult to be noticed. Amazon places a great deal of value on reviews, but statistically there is only one review written for every thousand books sold on Amazon. Some people stack the deck in their favor by having their friends write 4- and 5-star reviews before their book is even published. This practice crowds out the rest of us since their books immediately go to the top of the list and stay there because others buy their books based on the reviews.

Legitimate reviews help everybody. They help others to find the best books and avoid the bad ones. They also help authors to learn what they are doing right and what they need to improve. I honestly want to write the best books that I possibly can, but without feedback I have no idea if I am accomplishing my mission. I love to share what I have learned and save others from the many hours of effort that it took me to learn those things. Clear communication has always been my goal but only you can tell me if I am succeeding.

So, if you found value here, please help others to find these books by writing a review.

Glossary: Photography Speak

Aberration   A deviation from the norm, or a defect in the characteristics of a lens.

Aperture   The opening in the Diaphragm of a Compound Lens through which the image must pass. A means of blocking unwanted light from reaching the Sensor.

APS (Advanced Photo System)   An obsolete 1996 Standard for higher quality camera film. It never caught on for a variety of reasons including the success of digital cameras.

APS-C   A Digital Sensor roughly the size of a frame of APS Classic film.

APS-H   A Digital Sensor roughly the size of a frame of APS High-Defintion film

Auto-Exposure   The camera automatically sets Aperture and Shutter Speed based on image details and exposure measurements from the camera's built-in exposure meter.

Auto-Focus   Camera automatically adjusts the focus based on the closest object that coincides with an activated focus point in the camera's viewer. The more focus points that the camera uses, the better the chances of proper focus.

Auto Lighting Optimizer   Adds contrast and definition to dark and flat images.

Bridge Camera   A camera that "bridges the gap" between Point-and-Shoot and DSLR cameras.

CCD (Charge Coupled Device)   Sensors commonly used in precision digital imaging applications for science and medicine. Less common in digital cameras.

Center-Weighted Metering AE   An exposure metering method that places more attention on the center of the frame.

CMOS (Complementary Metal-Oxide-Semiconductor)   The type of Sensor that dominates the Digital camera market.

Color Space   A range of possible colors captured by digital cameras and displayed by monitors. Also, a range of colors that can be printed.

Color Temperature   A temperature scale related to the warmth or coldness of a lighting source. Common lighting sources have specific value ranges on this scale.

Compact System Camera   A Compact Camera with interchangeable Lenses.

Compound Lens   A collection of simple lenses that share a common axis to improve and focus the image passing through the Lens and onto the film or Sensor. The type of Lens assembly implied when a Photographer refers to his or her Lens.

Contact Prints   A process by which glass photographic negatives are placed in contact with light-sensitive photo paper and exposed to a burst of light. The photo paper is then treated in trays of chemicals to develop the image.

Cropping Factor   The ratio of the Diagonal Measurement of a given Sensor to the Diagonal Measurement of a Full-Frame Sensor.

Curtain Shutter   The type of Shutter used in SLR cameras – both film and digital. Two horizontal blades (curtains) that move vertically to expose the sensor or film.

Custom White Balance   A camera setting based on a Neutral (18%) Gray Card or its equivalent, used to establish the proper White balance or Color Temperature for a given lighting condition.

Darkroom   A dedicated light-proof room in which film negatives and prints are processed in trays of chemical solutions. During the process, the only light in the room is a dim red bulb.

Diaphragm   A device made up of several moveable blades that move in tandem to form and size the Aperture. It functions very much like the Iris of the human eye. It is usually sandwiched between two of the simple lenses that form a compound lens.

DIGIC (**DIG**ital **I**maging **C**ore)   Canon's Imaging Core Processor. Analogous to a computer's CPU.

Digital Camera   A camera in which the image is recorded by a photosensitive electronic SENSOR.

Digital SLR / DSLR   An SLR Camera in which the image is recorded by an electronic Sensor.

Effective Focal Length   Focal Length X Cropping Factor of Sensor being used.

Evaluative Metering AE (Auto-Exposure)   An exposure meter setting that divides the frame into several zones. Those zones are then used to calculate an average tonal value that can be related to an exposure setting.

EXPEED   Nikon's Imaging Core Processor.

Exposure Compensation   An adjustment on Digital cameras used to compensate for shortcomings of the camera's built-in exposure meter.

Exposure Triangle   Aperture, Shutter Speed, and ISO settings. These factors determine the amount of light that the Sensor requires to produce a properly exposed image.

File Compression   A process of reducing the file size while maintaining critical data.

Film Camera   A camera in which the image is recorded on photographic film.

Focal Length   The distance from the midplane of a lens to the focal point of the same lens. Usually measured in millimeters (mm).

Focal Plane   A Plane parallel to the midplane of a lens, also containing the Focal Point. Photographic film and Sensors are in this plane.

Focal Point   A point at which the light passing through a lens converges.

Frame (noun)   A portion of a roll of film that contains one image.

Frame (verb)   To limit the amount of the scene that will be captured by the camera. A step in composing an image.

Front Standard   A moveable frame in Large-Format Cameras that holds the Lens. It can be tilted in several directions relative to the Rear Standard. It can also be moved vertically relative to the Rear Standard.

Highlight Tone Priority   Preserves details in the bright areas of an image at the expense of the shadow areas.

Imaging Core   The Digital Camera equivalent of a computer's CPU.

Jpeg (Joint Photographic Experts Group)   A file format for photographic images that creates compressed files for easy and rapid transmission over the Internet and on Webpages.

Kit Lens   The Interchangeable Lens that is offered at the time of purchase with the camera body for DSLR cameras. There is often a choice of Kit Lenses at different price points. Purchasing a Lens with the camera body often represents a savings of several hundred dollars.

Large-Format Camera   A camera that captures an image on film or digital sensor that is larger than 4 in. X 5 in.

LCD (liquid Crystal Display) Screen   A small electronic display panel on the back of digital cameras used to display camera settings and review images.

Leaf Shutter   A type of shutter used in digital Point-and-Shoot cameras as well as Medium- and Large-Format cameras. It operates very much like the Diaphragm but is either wide open or totally closed.

Lens Extender Tube   A cylindrical tube that is mounted between a Lens and the Camera Body. Its purpose is to change the focal length of the Lens by a specified factor, for example, 1.4X.

Macro Lens   A Lens that is specifically designed for close-up photography of small subjects, such as flowers and bugs.

Medium-Format Camera   A camera that captures an image on film or digital sensor that is larger than 2.25 in. X 2.25 in. but less than 4in X 5 in

Mirror   A mirror which is normally in a 45° position to deflect the image coming through the camera lens to the Viewfinder. It snaps to a horizontal position just before the shutter opens and returns to its normal position just after the shutter closes. It can also be manually moved to the horizontal position for cleaning the Sensor and very fast exposures.

Mirrorless Camera   A Compact camera design with interchangeable Lenses that has no Mirror or Optical Viewfinder. Also known as an EVIL (Electronic Viewfinder Interchangeable Lenses) camera. This is somewhat misleading since most of these cameras have no Viewfinder at all – only an LCD Screen.

Negative   A photographic master print from which Positive (Normal) Prints are made. The tonal values are the exact opposite of the Positive or Print. In other words, white appears as black on the negative and black appears as white. Negatives can be glass plates, photographic film, or digital files.

Neutral Density Filters   A type of filter that screws onto the front of camera lenses. These filters are gray glass that has no effect on color but reduces the amount of light entering the lens. They are rated in *stops* so that they can easily be used to change exposure. They are often used in bright sunlight to allow for longer Shutter Speeds or larger Aperture Settings.

Neutral Gray Card   An 18% gray card that is sometimes used to set White Balance. It is difficult to define pure black or white, but easy to establish a shade of gray.

Partial Metering AE   Exposure based on 9% of the frame and located in the center of the frame.

Pentaprism   A special type of lens that is unique to SLR Cameras, and whose only purpose is to flip the image coming through the lens so that it can be observed right-side-up through the Viewfinder.

Photosite   A specific location on a photographic sensor where photons of a particular color of light are collected, counted, and recorded.

Pixel   A PIcture ELement or point of measureable color intensity and tone that is one element of a Mosaic-like image composed of many such elements – often in the millions.

Prime Lens   A Lens that has a fixed Focal Length. It has no Zoom capability.

RAW   A file format for photographic images that saves ALL the image data that the camera is capable of recording.

Rear Standard   A moveable frame in Large-Format Cameras that holds the photographic media – glass plate, film, or digital Sensor.

Remote Shutter Release   A device that allows the photographer to activate the shutter release without actually touching the camera. This is one way to reduce camera shake.

Sensor   An electronic device which captures and records photons of light and translates color and quantity of light data to Pixels that then form an image.

Shutter   A device whose purpose is to block light from the photographic recording medium except when an image is being captured. It opens and closes like the blink of an eye.

Simple Lens   A single piece of glass or plastic that refracts (bends) light in such a way that it converges to a point or diverges in a diffuse manner.

SLR (Single Lens Reflex) Camera   A particular style of camera that allows the photographer to look through the lens to compose his image. It contains a moveable mirror to deflect the image to the viewfinder and a Pentaprism to flip it right-side-up. SLRs also use interchangeable lenses.

Spot Metering AE   An exposure setting based on a small circle at the center of the frame – approximately 3.5% of the total area of the frame. Often used to properly expose a person's face when there is a bright background.

System Camera   A camera that can be modified by changing its components.

Tilt-Shift Lens   A Lens that can be Tilted or Shifted relative to the Sensor so that it changes normal perspective. Used to eliminate normal perspective distortions that are common in regular lenses. Performs the same function as the adjustments for the Front-Standard in a Large-Format View Camera.

View Angle   The angular expanse of the area visible through the viewfinder for a particular lens. It can be measured horizontally, vertically, or diagonally.

Viewfinder   A device that allows the photographer to view and compose his image.

White Balance   Color calibration for digital cameras based on light source. Standard settings include Daylight, Shade, Fluorescent, and other typical light sources. Most accurately set using an 18% neutral gray card.

The Following Definitions are LENS-Manufacturer Specific and therefore, no additional terms will be defined.

Canon Lenses

DO (Diffractive Optics)   Compacts glass elements while keeping chromatic aberration at a minimum. An example is Canon's EF 70-300 mm DO lens which is relatively small and light when compared to lenses with a similar zoom range.

DW-R (Dust and Water Resistant)   Most L-series lenses have this construction which allows for shooting in rainy and snowy weather as well as other harsh conditions, such as sandy beaches or humid jungles.

FP (Focus Preset)   Focus distance is preset and instantly returned to.

FT-M (Full Time Manual focus)   Manual Focus adjustments can be made even when Autofocus is engaged.

IS – (Image Stabilizer)   Employs a series of sensors and a high-speed microcomputer to measure the vibrations and apply corrections with a specialized lens group. Most useful when shooting hand-held at low light. Should be turned off when using a tripod. IS on/off switch is located on the body of a lens.

I/R (Inner and Rear Focusing)   Focusing is accomplished with the movement of internal lens groups, eradicating extension and rotation of the front lens element. This creates improved compactness and eases filter use.

L-series (Luxury)   Canon's top-of-the-line lenses. Identified by a red line around the front element of the lens. Image quality is second to none. Typically, heavy and expensive.

Macro Lenses   Can focus at extremely close distances.

STM – (Stepper Motor)   Used for focusing during video recording. Better than USM at producing smooth, precise, incremental movements needed for video capture, but slower at focusing during photo capture.

TS-E (Tilt-Shift with an electromagnetic diaphragm)   Moves Focal Plane to control perspective and Depth-of-Field. Manual focus only.

USM – (Ultrasonic motor)   Autofocus faster and quieter than AF lenses. Also draws less power from the camera than AF lenses.

Nikon (Nikkor) Lenses

AF   Autofocus.

AF-I (Auto Focus-Internal)   Found in older Nikkor lenses and is inferior to AF-S system.

AF-S (Auto Focus – Silent)   Uses "Silent Wave Motor" which focuses faster and quieter than typical AF lenses. Equivalent to Canon's USM system.

CRC (Close-Range Correction)   Lens elements can move independently resulting in better focusing ability at close distances.

D (Distance/Dimension)   Conveys focus distance information to camera's computer which then calculates correct exposure. Not supported by all Nikon Cameras.

DX Mount   For use on cameras with APS-C sized sensors. Is typically cheaper, smaller, and lighter than FX Lenses. Fits Cropped-Frame Cameras only.

ED (Extra-low Dispersion)   Minimizes chromatic aberration while effectively improving color correction and sharpness.

FX (F-mount)   For use on Full-Frame Cameras. Will fit any Canon SLR.

G   Must be used with Nikon DSLR body that can adjust lens aperture via the camera's command dial.

IF (Internal Focusing)   Similar to Canon's I/R system. Found in most modern Nikon's telephoto and zoom lenses.

Micro   For macro photography.

N (Nano Crystal Coat)   Internal elements coated with a nano crystal solution which eliminates reflections created by most wavelengths. This produces better quality images.

PC-E (Perspective Control with an electromagnetic diaphragm)
Similar to Canon's TS-E lenses.

RF (Rear Focusing)   Creates improved compactness.

SIC (Super Integrated Coating)   Multilayer coating minimizes lens flare and ghosting.

SWM (Silent Wave Motor)   Uses ultrasonic traveling waves during lens autofocus process.

VR (Vibration Reduction)   Similar to Canon's Image Stabilization (IS) system.

Sigma Lenses:

APO (Apochromatic)   Similar to Nikon's ED technology.

APS (Aspherical)   Similar to Canon's DO.

DC   For cameras with APS-C sized sensors. Like Canon's EF-S and Nikon's DX mounts.

DG   Similar to Canon's EF and Nikon's FX mounts.

DN   For use with mirrorless interchangeable lens cameras and will not fit typical SLRs.

EX (Excellence)   Similar to Canon's L lenses.

HF (Helical Focusing)   Keeps front element of a lens from rotating. Especially useful when using filters.

HSM (HyperSonic Motor)   Similar to Canon's USM and Nikon's AF-S systems.

OS (Optical Stabilization)   Similar to Canon's IS and Nikon's VR functions.

RF and IF   Comparable to Canon's I/R and Nikon's IF technologies.

Tamron lenses:

Di (Digitally Integrated)   Similar to Sigma DG

Di II   Similar to Sigma DC

Di III   Similar to Sigma DN

IF   Internal Focusing.

LD   Low Dispersion elements.

PZD (Piezo Drive)   Similar to Sigma HSM

SP (Super Performance)   Similar to Canon's L lenses.

USD (Ultrasonic Silent Drive)   Like Canon's USM and Nikon's AF-S technologies.

VC (Vibration Compensation)   Comparable to Canon's IS and Nikon's VR.

Tokina Lenses:

AS (Aspherical Optics)   Corrects for aspherical aberration as well as light quality and distortion.

AT-FX   Similar to Canon's EF and Nikon's FX mounts.

AT-X Pro   A line of lenses created with extra attention to quality for professionals.

DX   Similar to Canon's EF-S and Nikon's DX mounts.

FC (Focus Clutch)   Allows for switching the lens between auto focus and manual focus modes.

FE (Floating Element)   Corrects astigmatism from minimum-focus distance to infinity.

F&R (Advanced Aspherical Optics)   Provides even illumination in the corners and correction of spherical aberration throughout the entire image.

HLD (High-Refraction and Low-Dispersion)   Helps to eliminate chromatic aberration in wide-angle lenses.

IF   Internal Focusing system.

MC (Multi-Coating)   Helps to eliminate lens elements' surface reflections improving image quality.

SD (Super-low Dispersion)   Eliminates chromatic aberration.

X   Lenses for typical consumers. Usually lighter and cheaper.

Zeiss Lenses:

T*   Indicates anti-reflective coating which improves image quality in numerous lighting conditions.

ZA   Compatible with Sony's Alpha mounts.

ZE   Compatible with Canon's EF mounts.

ZF.2   Compatible with Nikon's F mounts.

pg. 136

Made in the USA
Monee, IL
20 April 2023

fde34628-a692-42e9-a14b-ca3484a78236R01